How to Win at Aptitude Tests

Volume II

By

Iain Maitland

Thorsons
An Imprint of HarperCollins*Publishers*

Thorsons
An Imprint of HarperCollins*Publishers*
77–85 Fulham Palace Road
Hammersmith, London W6 8JB

Published by Thorsons 1997

10 9 8 7 6 5 4 3 2

Iain Maitland asserts the moral right to
be identified as the author of this work

A catalogue record for this book is available
from the British Library

ISBN 0 7225 3261 X

Printed and bound in Great Britain by
Caledonian International Book Manufacturing Ltd, Glasgow

Contents

Acknowledgements

I wish to acknowledge the help and assistance of the
following organizations and individuals in the compilation of
this book:

- Imperial Chemicals Industries PLC

- Mensa

- Metropolitan Police

- NFER-Nelson Publishing Company Limited,
  and Robert Feltham in particular

- Savile Holdsworth.

Introduction

Whether you are looking for a new job or for a promotion, you may find yourself being asked to take an aptitude test. Not surprisingly, you will want to know as much as possible about these tests. What are they? What do they involve? How can I prepare properly, and succeed? This book answers these questions, and many more.

Chapter 1 'Understanding Aptitude Tests' discusses why tests are used during recruitment, transfer and promotion procedures, and sets out with examples the different types of test that exist, paying particular attention to those for verbal, non-verbal, numerical and spatial ability. It also explains how to prepare for these tests, which mainly involves practising on similar materials under comparable test conditions, and how to sit them successfully.

Chapters 2, 3, 4 and 5 look at each of the leading types of aptitude questions in turn: verbal, non-verbal, numerical and spatial ability. The key characteristics of those questions are detailed and supported by as wide a range of examples as you are likely to face. You can read through these questions for information purposes or even use them as mock tests, subsequently referring to the answers that follow. It is up to you.

Chapter 6 lists the answers to all of the questions that were given in Chapters 2, 3, 4 and 5. These answers and, where appropriate, the accompanying explanations not only help you to solve the questions but also to gain a better understanding of them. Read this chapter carefully.

Written in a down-to-earth, authoritative style and supported by illustrations, model questions and answers, tactical tips and chapter summaries, this book contains everything you need to know about aptitude tests, and more. It makes essential reading for anyone who wants to be offered that job, transfer or promotion.

1

Understanding Aptitude Tests

So what exactly is an 'aptitude test'? In theory, it can be defined as 'a process whereby a person's general intelligence and/or specific abilities are assessed objectively under controlled conditions'. In practice, it usually involves a person sitting at a desk providing written answers to a set number of multiple-choice questions in a relatively short period of time. Such tests are used with increasing frequency nowadays, as part of firms' recruitment, transfer and promotion procedures. If you are going to have to tackle an aptitude test (or a series of tests) then you must discover as much as possible about them – in particular, why they are used, the different types of aptitude test that exist, and how to prepare for and sit them successfully.

Using Tests

All types of businesses – large and small, and across many and varied trades and industries – now utilize aptitude tests to help them select the right people for jobs within their organizations. The reasons why tests are used more and more often these days can be understood by considering their benefits. Aptitude tests have drawbacks, too, which we shall also examine.

Benefits

Tests offer several benefits both to the firm incorporating them within their procedures, and to the candidates who sit them. Primarily, they act as an aid when making the selection decision. The recruitment process in most companies normally comprises a similar sequence of steps – application forms are sent out, completed, returned and appraised; interviews are conducted between candidates and a personnel manager (or whoever is responsible for filling the particular job); and referees' names and details are given, and references taken up before the final decision is made. Tests simply produce additional, and perhaps different, information to be taken into account – and the more information that is available, the better the final decision is likely to be.

Aptitude tests are also objective. The results are compared with 'averages' based on the performances of hundreds, or even thousands, of other people who have completed them in the past. Too often, application forms are screened, interviews are conducted and references are read subjectively, with information being interpreted according to personal opinion, and even likes and dislikes. Clearly, a reasoned, scientific approach to selecting people for jobs should generate more accurate and reliable results.

Tests can also provide a fuller, more comprehensive picture of candidates. General intelligence and certain specific abilities, such as being able to see three-dimensional objects from scale drawings, are hard to evaluate by application form, interview or reference alone. Similarly, tests can sometimes confirm the presence (or absence) of other abilities, such as spelling. After all, application forms may have been written with assistance, 'best' rather than realistic behaviour is seen at interviews and references might have been couched in vague rather than clear and concise language. With tests, hard, factual evidence is produced.

For businesses, testing helps to reduce the likelihood of the wrong person being chosen for a job, and all of the problems which that entails – inadequate workrate and performance, ill feeling amongst employees and, ultimately, dismissal, followed by re-recruitment. The costs of these – in terms of time, effort and money – are potentially enormous. For candidates, testing indicates that the firm takes recruitment very seriously indeed, and offers everyone an equal chance to succeed, with the possibility of someone being picked simply because they are a smooth-talking interviewee, for example, being much reduced, or even eliminated.

Drawbacks

Tests do have various drawbacks too – in particular, they are a highly specialized and skilled area of activity. Reputable tests take years to be developed, tested and checked to ensure they are both valid and reliable. 'Valid' means that they measure what needs to be measured, and do so accurately. 'Reliable' means that they are free from ambiguous questions that may be interpreted in different ways, by candidates and/or employers. Those who devise or run other, professionally designed, tests need to be fully trained and experienced if they are to produce meaningful tests and/or results. Otherwise, the likelihood of picking the wrong person is much increased.

They are also expensive. As a rough and ready example, if a firm decided to use tests as part of its selection process for filling clerical jobs and approached a test supplier for assistance, it might pay £1500 upwards for one of its managers to attend a training course enabling him or her to administer, score and interpret just one particular test. £200 or more might then need to be paid for manuals, guides, test sheets, answer booklets and scoring charts for 12 candidates to sit that test. Taking account, too, of the time and effort involved in running tests, it is clear that this is a costly exercise.

These drawbacks are outweighed by the benefits. For business organizations, aptitude tests produce valid and reliable results, untainted by personal feelings and guesswork. For people seeking a job, transfer or promotion, the fact that so much money is being spent to get the right person is reassuring.

Types of Aptitude Test

'General aptitude' tests, also known as 'general intelligence' and 'mental ability' tests, measure a candidate's basic intelligence, often in terms of verbal, non-verbal, numerical and spatial abilities. With a mix of words, symbols, numbers and shapes, the candidate may be asked to find a missing word (TEA _____ BOARD), continue a series of numbers (4, 9, 19, 39, _____) or do something similar. A set number of questions is usually tackled in a given period, perhaps twenty minutes.

'Specific aptitude', or 'special ability' tests, look at a candidate's particular talents, more often than not specific verbal, non-verbal, numerical and spatial abilities, possibly in such areas as spelling, verbal checking and numerical estimation. As examples, a report may need to be studied for spelling mistakes, a handwritten draft and its corresponding typed letter checked for errors and a set of figures for a sales projection added up and estimated totals provided for each of them. Once more, a number of questions will have to be answered in a short space of time, perhaps up to thirty minutes. The best way of gaining a fuller understanding of aptitude tests is to contemplate:

- verbal ability questions
- non-verbal ability questions
- numerical ability questions
- spatial ability questions.

Verbal Ability Questions

These questions involve words and are designed to show how well you understand and deal with verbal concepts and ideas. At a general level, you will most often be asked to find a missing word and identify the odd word out from amongst several, which may indicate how intelligent you are. More specific tests of verbal ability can be set too. Spelling questions may be incorporated if you have to draft or write memos, letters or reports as part of the job. Word meanings evaluate the range and depth of your vocabulary – helpful if the job entails spotting errors in notices, mailshots and the like. Verbal checking assesses your speed and accuracy at cross-referencing, which is useful if you have to check lists, minutes and so on in the job.

Here are some example questions and answers.

Example: Finding a Missing Word
You have to find a word which can be placed between the words shown to produce two new words.

Question: Foot _____ Point
Answer: Ball (Football .... Ballpoint)

Example: Identifying the Odd Word Out
Circle the odd one out amongst the following six words.

Question: Apple Lemon Peach Grape Raspberry Orange
Answer: Peach (It is the only one with a stone.)

Example: Spelling
Underline the correct spelling of the following word.

Question:
Permanent Permenent Permenant Permanant Permannent
Answer: Permanent

Example: Word Meanings
Which of the five words on the right means (almost) the same as the one on the left.

Question: Maim – Scare Injure Kill Destroy Frighten
Answer: Injure

Example: Verbal Checking

Circle any differences in these lists.

Question:

1.	A. J. Bannen	1.	A. J. Bannen
2.	M. P. Hardcastle	2.	M. P. Hardcastle
3.	P. P. Kingsmere	3.	P. P. Kingmere
4.	F. L. Marvin	4.	F. L. Marven
5.	T. R. Quincy	5.	T. P. Quincy

Answer:

1.	A. J. Bannen	1.	A. J. Bannen
2.	M. P. Hardcastle	2.	M. P. Hardcastle
3.	P. P. Kingsmere	3.	P. P. Kin(gm)ere
4.	F. L. Marvin	4.	F. L. Marv(en)
5.	T. R. Quincy	5.	T.(P.) Quincy

Non-verbal Ability Questions

These questions are based upon symbols and are used to evaluate your ability to process and differentiate between relevant and irrelevant data, and to think in an abstract manner. Typically, you will have to match symbols, spot the odd symbol out and continue a series of symbols in a logical way. Often, non-verbal ability questions vary quite considerably in their degree of complexity and difficulty, as can be seen in these example questions and answers.

Example: Matching Symbols

Question: Identify the matching symbol by underlining the appropriate letter.

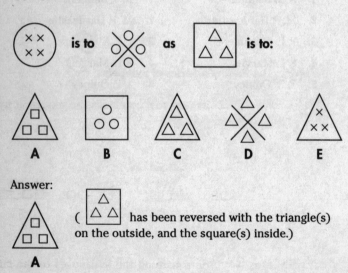

Answer:

(has been reversed with the triangle(s) on the outside, and the square(s) inside.)

A

Example: Spot the Odd Symbol Out

Question: Spot the odd symbol out by circling the letter beneath it.

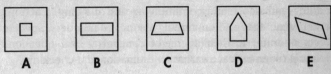

A   **B**   **C**   **D**   **E**

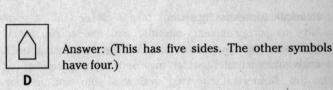

D

Answer: (This has five sides. The other symbols have four.)

Example: Continuing a Series of Symbols

Question: Identify the symbol that continues the sequence, by underlining the letter below.

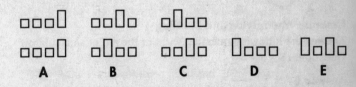

A   **B**   **C**   **D**   **E**

☐☐☐☐
D

Answer: (The square on the left moves to the far right at each stage.)

Numerical Ability Questions

Questions of this nature include numbers and are constructed to show how well you reason with figures. Those that might arise in a general intelligence test will probably focus on adding and subtracting, multiplying and dividing, fractions and percentages and continuing a series of numbers. Specific tests of numerical ability might concentrate on questions relating to numerical awareness, estimation and checking.

Numerical awareness questions take a closer look at your ability to add, subtract, multiply and divide. Numerical estimation appraises your potential for estimating both quickly and accurately, which may be a key requirement for the job. Numerical checking evaluates your aptitude for spotting errors in handwritten and printed data. Here are various example questions and answers.

Example: Adding and Subtracting
Do the following calculation, without using a calculator.
Question: 295 – 97 + 123 – 33 + 17 =

Answer: 305

Example: Multiplying and Dividing
Answer the following question without the aid of a calculator.
Question: $18 \times 9 \div 3 =$

Answer: 54

Example: Fractions and Percentages
Calculate the following.
Question: $\frac{1}{3} + \frac{2}{3} + \frac{2}{9} =$

Answer: $1 \frac{2}{9}$ ($\frac{3}{9} + \frac{6}{9} + \frac{2}{9} = \frac{11}{9}$)

Question: 6% of 75 =

Answer: 4.5

Example: Continuing a Series of Numbers
Complete this sequence of numbers.

Question: 7 12 16 19 21 ____

Answer: 22 (Numbers increase at a decreasing rate: +5, +4, +3, +2, +1.)

Example: Numerical Awareness
Circle any mistakes in these calculations, and put in the correct figures next to them.

Question:

2	×	AZ4031	@	£9.99	=	£19.98	
3	×	AM6266	@	£7.99	=	£22.97	
3	×	AF3371	@	£8.99	=	£26.97	
5	×	AQ7436	@	£7.95	=	£39.77	
						£109.69	

Answer:

2	×	AZ4031	@	£9.99	=	£19.98	
3	×	AM6266	@	£7.99	=	(£22.97)	£23.97
3	×	AF3371	@	£8.99	=	£26.97	
5	×	AQ7436	@	£7.95	=	(£39.77)	£39.75
						(£109.69)	£110.67

Example: Numerical Estimation
Calculate the following, placing a cross (X) in the box representing the figure that is nearest to your answer.

Question: A man walks 3.5 miles per hour for five hours each day. How long would it take him to complete a 127-mile journey?

5 days ☐

6 days ☐

7 days ☐

8 days ☐

9 days ☐

10 days ☐

Answer: 7 days ☒ (3.5 miles per hour × 5 hours per day = 17.5 miles per day. 127 miles ÷ 17.5 miles per day = 7.26 days)

Example: Numerical Checking
Circle any differences in these lists.

Question:

1.	378963/43	**1.**	378963/47
2.	949494/46	**2.**	944949/46
3.	327272/77	**3.**	327272/77
4.	411114/31	**4.**	411144/31
5.	696692/26	**5.**	696992/26

Answer:

1. 378963/43	1. 378963/47
2. 949494/46	2. 944949/46
3. 327272/77	3. 327272/77
4. 411114/31	4. 411144/31
5. 696692/26	5. 696992/26

Spatial Ability Questions

Your spatial ability – or lack of it – may be estimated by the way in which you answer questions involving shapes. Typically, you will have to fit shapes together, imagine how a flattened shape would appear when folded to create a solid object and visualize how a solid object would look when unfolded. Sometimes, spatial ability questions can be quite diverse in nature, as may be seen by these example questions and answers.

Example: Fitting Shapes Together

Identify the shapes which fit together by underlining the appropriate letter.

Question:

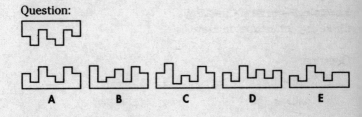

A B C D E

Answer:

A

13

Example: Creating Solid Objects

Question: Identify the solid object created by folding together the flat pattern, by circling the relevant letter.

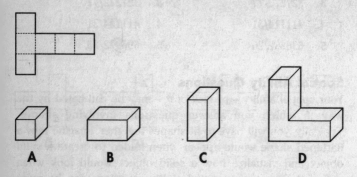

A **B** **C** **D**

Answer:

(A)

Example: Unfolding Solid Objects

Question: Indicate how the solid object will look unfolded, by underlining the appropriate letter.

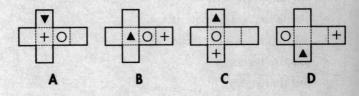

A   **B**   **C**   **D**

Answer:

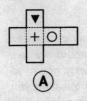

(A)

Preparing for Tests

You may have applied recently for a job, transfer or promotion, had an interview and been told that you now need to sit an aptitude test along with several other of the better candidates for the position. Your preparations for this should comprise the following, key steps:

- find out about the test
- obtain similar test materials
- plan a timetable of practice
- practise regularly
- rest thoroughly
- attend the test.

Find Out about the Test

An obvious point perhaps – but one which many candidates overlook – is to discover as much as possible about the test you are going to have to tackle. To prepare properly, you need to know what the test will involve, the types of question you will face and how long it will last. Clearly, you must ask the firm to provide you with this information. Most will be obliging, with some supplying literature such as the GAT Test Taker's Guide (see below) which you should study carefully.

General Ability Tests
A Test Taker's Guide

This is reproduced with the kind permission of ASE, a division of the NFER-Nelson Publishing Company Limited.

You may have been sent this leaflet to help you prepare for your testing session. It:

- introduces you to the tests themselves;
- gives you an idea of what to expect;
- provides hints on how to prepare yourself;
- answers key questions; but remember that you can still ask questions at the testing session.

Here are the answers to some important questions.

Q   Why am I being asked to take some tests?

A   You may have school or work qualifications, but these tests give extra information which will help employers to select those applicants who are best suited to the job or their training programme.

Tests also help you to explore your abilities; this should assist you in choosing a suitable area of work.

People who are successful in the job have usually done well in the tests, so both employers and applicants get what they want.

Q   How do they work?

A   Employers decide which skills and abilities are needed in the job. Tests are then selected to measure some of these.
There is a practice period in the testing session to make sure everyone understands how to do the test(s).
The tests are carefully timed, so you may not finish; but you should work as fast as you can and follow the instructions given.
Your answers are then scored and this information is used to help decide whether you will be suitable for the job.

Q   Will I be asked to do anything else?

A   Usually you will be asked to fill in an application form and this information is also very important.
You may also be interviewed. Employers use information from many sources to help them make the best decision.

The Test Session

When you come to the session you will be asked to do the tests ticked below. The time shown beside each test is the time you will be allowed once you have been given the introductory examples and practice test. Remember you will be given a break between the tests.

- Verbal   15 minutes
- Numerical   20 minutes
- Non-Verbal   20 minutes
- Spatial   20 minutes

Look at the examples given for each of the tests you will be taking. None of these examples will be in the real tests. Check that you understand the questions and correct answers. Remember that if you do not understand there will be time to ask before the test begins.

The Answer Sheet

You will be given a separate answer sheet for each test. The one given below is from the Verbal Test and is marked with the correct answers for the examples given. The Numerical and Non-Verbal answer sheets are very similar.

1	A	B	C	D	E	F
2	A	B	C	D	E	F
3	A	B	C	D	E	F
4	A	B	C	D	E	F
5	A	B	C	D	E	F
6	A	B	C	D	E	F

13	A	B	C	D	E	F
14	A	B	C	D	E	F
15	A	B	C	D	E	F
16	A	B	C	D	E	F
17	A	B	C	D	E	F
18	A	B	C	D	E	F

25	A	B	C	D	E	F
26	A	B	C	D	E	F
27	A	B	C	D	E	F
28	A	B	C	D	E	F
29	A	B	C	D	E	F
30	A	B	C	D	E	F

Below is a section from the Spatial answer sheet. The correct answers to Example 1 to 4 are marked.

1	Y	N	17	Y	N	33	Y	N	49	Y	N	65	Y	N
2	Y	N	18	Y	N	34	Y	N	50	Y	N	66	Y	N
3	Y	N	19	Y	N	35	Y	N	51	Y	N	67	Y	N
4	Y	N	20	Y	N	36	Y	N	52	Y	N	68	Y	N
5	Y	N	21	Y	N	37	Y	N	53	Y	N	69	Y	N
6	Y	N	22	Y	N	38	Y	N	54	Y	N	70	Y	N
7	Y	N	23	Y	N	39	Y	N	55	Y	N	71	Y	N
8	Y	N	24	Y	N	40	Y	N	56	Y	N	72	Y	N

Verbal

This test is about relationships between pairs of words. In each question you are given one pair of words and you have to find out how they are related. Then you have to choose a word, from the six given, which would complete another pair of words. The missing word is shown by a question mark. The second pair must be related to each other in the same way as the pair you have been given.

In the two examples below the correct answers are highlighted: **'clothes'** is the answer to Example 1, and **'line'** is the answer to Example 2.

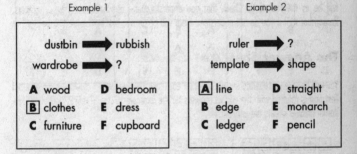

Example 1

dustbin ➡ rubbish

wardrobe ➡ ?

A wood   D bedroom
B clothes E dress
C furniture F cupboard

Example 2

ruler ➡ ?

template ➡ shape

A line   D straight
B edge   E monarch
C ledger F pencil

Non-verbal

In this test you have to work out relationships between shapes. There are two basic types of question. In the first, as Example 1, you are given two large figures inside an oval. You have to decide how they are alike, which may be in one way or several ways. Only one figure at the bottom also has all these qualities. In this case there is a small shape followed by a dotted line, then two solid lines. Only figure **'A'** fits this description. The correct answer has been highlighted.

In the other questions, such as Examples 2 and 3, there is a grid which contains an arrangement of shapes with one missing section. This is marked by the question mark. You have to decide how the shapes are related to each other and decide which of the six possibilities is the missing one.

In Example 2, the three figures in the centre of each big triangle are repeated in the outer triangles next to them. Also, each repeated figure has either a circle or a triangle around it. Here, the answer is **'F'**.

In Example 3, a different grid is used. The answer, which is **'A'**, can be found by looking at the pattern of shapes in the inside and outside triangles.

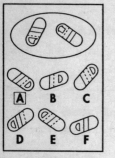

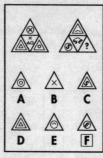

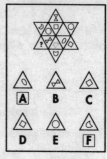

| Example 1 | Example 2 | Example 3 |

Numerical

In this test you have to work out the relationship between numbers. All questions have an arrangement of numbers in a grid with one or two numbers missing. The missing numbers are shown by question marks. You have to find how the numbers are related to each other and so decide which of the six possibilities is the missing one.

If you look at the first example below, the numbers in the 'chain' on the left-hand side go in sequence by 'doubling up'. Thus, twice 3 is 6; twice 6 is 12; and twice 12 is 24. Therefore the missing answer is **24** or **'C'**. The correct answer has been highlighted.

Sometimes you have two numbers missing and you will have to find the answer which has them both. In Example 2 you have to look across the rows and down the columns rather like a crossword. Going across the rows, the numbers increase by the same amount; going down the rows they double each time. You must find the two numbers that fit both of these rules. The missing numbers are **14** and **20**, which is answer **'A'**.

In Example 3, you again must find the two missing numbers. Here, the bottom number on the left is always 21 more than the top number, and the one on the right is always 10 more than the top numbers. Thus, the correct answer is **'A'**.

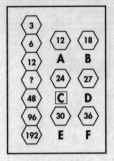

Example 1

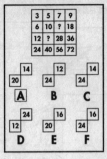

Example 2

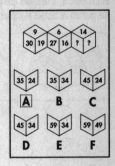

Example 3

Spatial

In this test you have to imagine what a flat pattern would look like if it were cut out and folded into a solid object. The patterns have to be folded along the black lines so that the markings are on the outside of the solid object.

You have to decide if each of the solid objects shown below the flat pattern could be made from it when folded. Answer 'no' if an object definitely **could not** be made and 'yes' if it definitely **could** be made. If you cannot be sure without seeing the hidden side, answer 'yes'.

In Example 1, if the pattern were folded it would form a long shape with one black side and the dot in the correct places. Similarly, the answer to question 2 is 'yes' since there is one black side and you can only see one of the ends; the other one could have the dot on it. However, the answer to question 3 is clearly 'no' since the long side on the top left should be black. Question 4 is 'yes' because the black side is hidden under the shape. The correct answers are under the questions.

In Example 2 the answers to questions 5, 6 and 7 are 'yes', while the answer to 8 is 'no'.

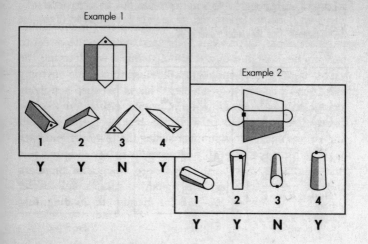

Example 1

1 2 3 4
Y Y N Y

Example 2

1 2 3 4
Y Y N Y

Q How can I prepare myself for the test?

- Prepare yourself by having a good night's sleep and arriving well in time.

- If you normally wear glasses or a hearing aid remember to bring them with you.

- Read this leaflet carefully and make sure you understand what to expect from the tests you will be doing.

Q How do I do my best in the tests?

- Don't be afraid to ask a question if there is something not clear to you.

- Listen carefully and follow the instructions given as well as you can.

- If it is a long time since you did an exam or test, do not worry! Test results, if used correctly, should give a fair assessment regardless of your age, race, sex or background.

Obtain Similar Test Materials

Ideally, you will ask the business for complete (or substantial parts of) copies of previous tests used and/or write direct to test suppliers for mock tests. Although this is worth trying, the vast majority of test suppliers will refuse to provide anything more than one or two examples. This is because supplying significant amounts of material would either breach the contractual agreement between the test user and supplier and/or prevent the test supplier selling the test over and over again in the future. After all, no firm wants to buy and use a test that candidates may have seen before. Reputable suppliers and users treat tests as closely guarded secrets. See 'Useful Contacts' on pages 179–181 for details of leading test suppliers.

Accumulating one or two examples from the business and perhaps half a dozen test suppliers, however, can help you build up some knowledge. Mensa – that well-known organization for intelligent people – provides tests for its (prospective) members and many of the questions in these could be categorized as general verbal, non-verbal, numerical and spatial in nature. This is another useful contact which you should approach. Magazines and books from your local newsagents, bookshop or library may incorporate questions, short or even full-length tests of a broadly comparable style to the ones you are facing. Check these out too. Refer to 'Further Reading' on pages 183–184 for information about various publications that may be of benefit to you.

Plan a Timetable of Practice

Sit down and plan out exactly when you are going to practise on any comparable test materials you have obtained. Always pace yourself so that you do a little each day for the week or so leading up to the test, rather than attempting to cram everything in the night before – that would inevitably make you feel tense and ill at ease. It is advisable to tackle your test materials in times and conditions which are as similar as possible to those you will face on the day – so set aside thirty minutes or whatever every day, and go somewhere quiet, where you can work undisturbed.

Practise Regularly
Without a doubt, sitting similar tests in comparable times and conditions and on a regular basis is the best way of practising. At the end of each mock test, look at the answers to see how you did – but do not be disappointed if you did not do as well as you had hoped first time around. After all, the purpose of practising is to learn from your mistakes and to improve your performance. Put each test aside for a few days and then come back to it to see if you do any better next time. Inevitably, you will.

Practice does not make perfect, whatever people might say, but it will help to produce improvements – enabling you to avoid obvious mistakes in future, to gain a fuller understanding of what you are doing and to work faster so that more (or even all) questions are completed in the time allowed. How much you improve will depend on numerous factors – not least your initial level of experience, the relevance of the material used and the amount of practice done – but you will benefit from it, often quite noticeably. Perhaps most important of all, you should gain in confidence, which will give you a distinct advantage over the other candidates.

Rest Thoroughly
You need to be at your best when you are tackling a series of quick-fire questions in a short period of time – and this means being fresh, alert and responsive. Have plenty of sleep the night before so that you wake up feeling mentally alert, and ready for action. Eat lightly at breakfast and at lunch, if

appropriate, as a heavy meal can make you feel uncomfortable and deaden your senses. Similarly, avoid drinking alcohol, fizzy drinks and coffee before a test as these can affect you adversely too, one way or another. Try to stay sharp and wide awake in the hours and minutes leading up to the test.

Attend the Test

Another obvious point, or so it seems. On average, however, as many as three out of every ten candidates invited to sit an aptitude test do not turn up on the day. So do attend, because your chances will be much better than you might have first estimated, simply because a number of your rivals will fail to arrive. The reasons for this are not always easy to identify conclusively – some may have decided they do not want this job for whatever reason, whilst others may be unavailable at that specific time, possibly unable to take time off from their current employment. Most likely, though, is that they have become overcome with nerves and tension, and just cannot face the occasion.

Do not worry too much – after all, you've survived this far, got through an interview and are almost there. You really have very little to be concerned about now. You will probably just have to sit quietly at a desk facing the person who interviewed you or a more experienced test administrator brought in for the occasion, spend 30 minutes or so in silence answering a paper full of questions similar to those reproduced in the following chapters, and that is about it. So gather up a supply of pens and pencils, a rubber and a pencil sharpener and get ready to go and succeed at that test!

Sitting Tests

Often, testing will take place at the same venue that you attended for an interview. You should prepare yourself for taking the tests as seriously and conscientiously as you did for the interview itself, paying careful attention to your appearance, arriving on time, and so on.

Regardless of whether you are sitting the test on your own or with other candidates, you will invariably have to do it at a desk, facing the administrator. To begin with, they will probably introduce themselves fully, explain the purpose of the test – in essence, to evaluate your suitability for this position – and tell you how long it will last. They should then outline carefully what you are expected to do – such as to answer the 60 multiple-choice questions in section one of the booklet within 30 minutes, circling the correct answers in pencil, working in silence, and so on. It is absolutely essential that you do precisely what you are told to do, if you want to succeed. The majority of candidates who reach this stage do not. They fail to listen properly and answer the wrong questions or the right ones in the wrong way – and consequently, they fail.

Sitting the tests can be divided into two, main stages: the practice session and the test itself.

The Practice Session
Many tests incorporate a practice session of perhaps five minutes or so which enables you – and the administrator – to check that you are doing what you ought to be doing. The practice material should include a set of instructions which will already have been summarized for you or possibly even read out to you word for word. It is important that you study these at least twice just to make certain you tackle the practice

test correctly. It cannot be stressed enough that many candidates fail because they think they know rather than actually know what they are doing. Take the practice material seriously, trying to answer the correct questions accurately, and in the time allowed. If you have misheard or misinterpreted an instruction this is your last – indeed, only – chance to put it right.

Following this practice, your paper and any others will be collected and looked at, whilst you and any fellow candidates take a break, either at your desks or in a waiting area. Wherever you are, attempt to relax and stay calm. Breathe deeply, focus on something cheerful and upbeat – like the end of the test! – and try not to worry about the mistakes you may have made. Easier said than done, but essential nonetheless. The reason for this dummy run is to ensure you are working along the right lines, not to label you a failure. Approach it accordingly, listening to and taking note of any comments made by the administrator, and get ready to complete the real test – and score high.

As an alternative to a practice session, the front of your test paper may simply state the instructions followed by a series of example questions and answers, similar to those shown in the GAT Test Taker's Guide (see pages 17–20). Look at these carefully, making sure you understand them. If you have prepared thoroughly – and tackled verbal, non-verbal, numerical and spatial ability questions – these should be very familiar to you. Read them at least twice to make absolutely certain that you really understand both the instructions that are being given, and how the answers to the various questions have been found.

If you have any queries about the test or any aspects of it, do raise them before the test begins. If you do not, no-one else will, and once the test is under way, it will be too late to resolve them. You may feel awkward and embarrassed about asking a question – and might even look foolish if the answer is an obvious one – but this is better than proceeding in ignorance, and doing the test completely wrong. With any questions answered and the test about to commence, carry out a final check to make sure that you have everything you need – question paper, answer sheet, rough paper, pen or pencil and a spare, rubber and pencil sharpener, as appropriate. Then wait to be given the go ahead, take a deep breath, turn over the page, and start.

The Test Itself

The dos and don'ts of actually sitting an aptitude test are fairly straightforward. As stressed, your primary concern must be to answer the correct questions in the right way – so do part one not part two, circle rather than underline, use pencil not pen, put a cross through a wrong answer and circle the right one, and so forth. It is easy to dismiss such advice as being painfully obvious, but as so many candidates fail because of such elementary mistakes, it needs to be stated over and again.

It is also important that you are conscious of the time constraints upon you – when practising you probably found it difficult to complete all the questions in the time permitted, and a similar situation may be experienced during the test itself. Stay calm and accept that this is a fairly common occurrence in most test situations – just keep thinking that if you do not have enough time, neither will your rival candidates. Concentrate on doing the best you can, which will be better than those less well-prepared candidates will be able to do. Whatever happens, do not panic and become flustered as this may mean you start to rush, misread questions and give the wrong answers.

Try to work efficiently and accurately too. Focus on those questions which you know you can answer correctly, working through them as swiftly as you can, rather than struggling through each and every question in turn, including those you find difficult or cannot understand. Do not waste your precious time on those questions you are likely to get wrong anyway. Come back to them towards the end if you have any time left, and spend a few minutes mulling over the answers. Have a guess if necessary, especially if there are multiple-choice answers – you probably have at least a one in five chance of making the correct choice, if not better odds as some answers will be obviously wrong. An extra mark here and there can make a significant difference to your final, over-all score.

Occasionally, you will complete all of the questions before the test comes to an end. If this happens, it is advisable to spend the remaining minutes going over the paper again and again, to spot mistakes, questions which you may have overlooked, and so on. Do not do what some arrogant and foolish candidates do – pushing the paper to one side, leaning back and looking smug and triumphant will not endear you to the administrator, or anyone else watching. Your time in this test is valuable so use it wisely to improve your score as far as possible.

Summary

1. An aptitude test is 'a process whereby a person's general intelligence and/or specific abilities are assessed objectively under controlled conditions'.

2. Aptitude tests are used with increasing frequency nowadays, and by all types of businesses. They offer various:

   a. benefits, such as objectivity and the ability to produce a fuller, more comprehensive picture of candidates

   b. drawbacks, such as their highly specialized nature and the costs of administrating them.

3. Numerous types of aptitude test exist. The most common ones include:

   a. verbal ability questions, involving words

   b. non-verbal ability questions, with symbols

   c. numerical ability questions, using numbers

   d. spatial ability questions, with shapes.

4. Successful candidates for a job, transfer or promotion prepare thoroughly for tests. This means:

   a. finding out about the test

   b. obtaining similar test materials to practise on

   c. planning a timetable of practice

   d. practising regularly

   e. resting thoroughly before the test

   f. attending the test.

5. Testing is often carried out at the same place that job interviews were held, and should be approached in an equally serious manner. The process normally consists of two stages:

   a. the practice session, to identify and remedy problems

   b. the test itself, full of verbal, non-verbal, numerical and spatial ability questions.

2

Verbal
Ability
Questions

These questions are concerned with words, and your answers
will indicate whether or not you have an aptitude for verbal
concepts and ideas. They may appear extensively in a general
intelligence test and/or in a more specific aptitude test. To
begin with, you should have some background knowledge of
the characteristics of these questions before looking at the
questions that follow, and their answers.

Characteristics

In a general intelligence test, verbal ability questions are most likely to involve such tasks as finding a missing word and identifying the odd word out. More specific tests might feature questions relating to spelling, word meanings and verbal checking, amongst others. This chapter gives numerous examples of a wide variety of verbal ability questions. You can either study these and read the accompanying tips at your own pace or approach them as a test. Whatever you do, be sure to check the answers in Chapter 6 to assess your understanding in this area.

Clearly, the best way of preparing for verbal ability questions is to tackle as many as you can, to think carefully about any tactical tips offered and to look at the answers to see how well you did, and where you went wrong. The examples which follow are grouped under these headings:

- finding a missing word
- identifying the odd word out
- spelling
- word meanings
- verbal checking.

Finding a Missing Word

Find the word which links the two words shown, writing it in the space provided. For example, play GROUND work.

1. note _____ clip
2. cat _____ jack
3. spine _____ on

4. paper _____ friend
5. clock _____ space
6. snow _____ handle
7. ball _____ less
8. mouse _____ door
9. play _____ knife
10. mid _____ end
11. high _____ lord
12. hose _____ dream
13. ran _____ cloth
14. bird _____ time
15. chain _____ dust

Tip

Probably the best way of approaching these questions is to take the first word and think of all the other words which develop from it. If the first word is 'note', for example, then you might think of 'notelet', 'notebook', 'notepaper', 'noteworthy' and so on. Running the second word after this should then indicate the answer – note-let-clip and note-book-clip are obviously nonsensical, whilst note-paper-clip sounds correct, and is.

Identifying the Odd Word Out

Discover the word which does not belong in the group of five shown. For example, narrate, recite, compose, relate, declaim. Underline the odd one out.

1. bridge, poker, pontoon, cribbage, whist
2. tea, coffee, milk, sugar, chocolate
3. shrimp, lobster, cray, crab, prawn
4. milk, bread, cheese, yoghurt, butter
5. box, helmet, goggles, pads, bat
6. budgerigar, parrot, canary, sparrow, lovebird
7. carrot, tomato, potato, turnip, onion
8. scare, frighten, intimidate, threaten, attack
9. joke, snigger, smirk, giggle, smile
10. march, tramp, walk, hike, run

Tip

Sometimes, the odd one out will leap off the page at you, although it is wise to check your thinking before underlining the answer. Usually, though, you will have to work at it. Instead of trying to spot the rogue word immediately, find links between the listed words until one stands alone, as the odd one out.

Spelling

Find the Correct Spelling

Circle the correct spelling of these words. As an example:

(a) receive   (b) receeve   (c) recieve

1. (a) occasional   (b) ocassional   (c) occassional
2. (a) exagerate   (b) exxagerate   (c) exaggerate
3. (a) fulfil   (b) fulfill   (c) fullfil
4. (a) ceiling   (b) cieling   (c) cealing
5. (a) parallel   (b) paralell   (c) parrallell
6. (a) rhythm   (b) ryhthm   (c) rythm
7. (a) dissapear   (b) disapear   (c) disappear
8. (a) acommodate   (b) accomodate   (c) accommodate
9. (a) susceptable   (b) susceptible   (c) suscepteble
10. (a) predudice   (b) prejudice   (c) predjudice
11. (a) embarrassment   (b) embarassment   (c) embarrasment
12. (a) commitee   (b) comittee   (c) committee
13. (a) compatable   (b) compatible   (c) compaterble
14. (a) temporary   (b) temparary   (c) temperary
15. (a) consencus   (b) concensus   (c) consensus
16. (a) disgracefull   (b) dissgraceful   (c) disgraceful
17. (a) preparation   (b) preperation   (c) preparetion
18. (a) benerficial   (b) beneficiall   (c) beneficial
19. (a) garanteed   (b) guaranteed   (c) guarunteed
20. (a) debatible   (b) debateable   (c) debatable

Plurals

Underline the correct spelling of the plural of the word shown.

For example:
> **Interview – interviewees, interviewes, <u>interviews</u>, interviewers, intervieweses**

21. Vacancy – vacancys, vacancees, vacanses, vacancyes, vacancies

22. Medium – mediums, media, mediumses, mediumes, medii

23. Roof – roofs, rooves, roovs, roofes, roofses

24. Ambiguity – ambiguities, ambiguitys, ambiguityes, ambiguitees, ambiguityses

25. Business – businessis, business, businesss, businesses, businessess

26. Taxi – taxies, taxes, taxise, taxises, taxis

27. Customer – customers, customeres, customerse, customerers, customurs

28. Shelf – shelves, shelfes, shelfs, shelvs, shelvses

29. Stadium – stadia, stadiums, stadiumes, staduim, stadiumses

30. Company – companies, companees, companyes, companieses, companys

37

Correct the Spelling Mistake

Read the following sentences, crossing out any words spelt incorrectly, and placing the correct spelling directly above them.

As an example: **except**
   Everyone attended the meeting, ~~accept~~ Michael James.

31.   The office was very quite this morning.

32.   I am to busy to do it today.

33.   The noise effected my concentration.

34.   I put the letter threw the letterbox.

35.   They say there cheque is in the post.

36.   There is a draft coming from that window.

37. We did not no that an order had been sent.

<figure>know</figure>

38. We will visit customers werever they are.

<figure>wherever</figure>

39. I switched of the computer when I finished working.

<figure>off</figure>

40. The local priest performed the last rites on the dying man.

<figure>rites</figure>

Tip

Sometimes, you will be given text to correct – either a series of sentences, or perhaps a memo, letter or report. Clearly, this can be harder than tackling a series of multiple-choice questions as the right answers are not in front of you. Here, you really need to be a good speller, capable of spelling every word correctly – no mean feat! Once more, saying sentences slowly in your head and writing them out may be useful. Also, be aware that some sentences will include one error, others two and a proportion none at all. So, don't make the mistake of trying to correct something which is already right!

Word Meanings

Synonyms

'Synonyms' are words which mean much the same as each other. As an example, a spot is a pimple, and vice versa. Circle the synonym for each of these words:

1. Delete – amend, erase, change, adjust, evaluate

2. Pied – dark, musical, intoxicated, dappled, colourful

3. Suave – urbane, slippery, oily, clever, handsome

4. Concise – organized, neat, succinct, detailed, explanatory

5. Repose – lean, erect, build, rest, fasten

6. Toxic – poisonous, powerful, inflammatory, evil, dangerous

7. Latent – loud, creamy, secret, misplaced, definite

8. Robust – tough, clean, hard, firm, vigorous

9. Profane – noisy, clear, obscene, unpleasant, unusual

10. Coarse – sharp, dirty, blunt, rough, lumpy

Antonyms

'Antonyms' are words that mean virtually the opposite of each other. For example, hot is the opposite of cold. Circle the antonym for each of these words:

11. Cautious – dangerous, impetuous, exciting, overpowering, exhilarating

12. Build – destroy, expand, refine, adjust, obscure

13. Pride – anger, greed, selfishness, humility, distress

14. Consent – agree, approve, dispute, argue, refuse

15. Variable – solid, exceptional, regular, occasional, unpredictable

16. Preface – introduction, text, amendments, acknowledgments, postscript

17. Pungent – mild, sticky, obscure, sharp, soft

18. Vivid – clear, ordinary, extreme, striking, dull

19. Reconcile – improve, alienate, widen, weaken, disapprove

20. Unique – odd, unusual, different, usual, compatible

Tip

In aptitude tests, antonym questions will often follow synonyms, so you need to bear in mind that you are now looking for *opposite* rather than *similar* words. Do not get confused! A good way of answering these questions correctly is to look at the original word, shut your eyes and think of the opposite word. Then see if this or something similar is listed, and circle it. If in doubt, exclude the similar words which are included to fool you and hazard a guess between the remaining possibilities.

Comparisons

'Comparisons' exist when two words are connected by a common link. You then have to look at a new word and find its comparison by using that same, common link. As an example, pitch is to football as piste is to skiing. Underline the comparison for each of the following:

21. 'Apple' is to 'Tree' as 'Rose' is to garden, bush, border, water, thorn

22. 'Nail' is to 'Clipper' as 'Hair' is to head, dye, cap, scissors, hat

23. 'Sour' is to 'Taste' as 'Odorous' is to mood, feeling, sound, smell, touch

24. 'Filament' is to 'Lightbulb' as 'Wick' is to lamp, wax, candle, gun, chimney

25. 'Paper' is to 'Wood' as 'Leather' is to skin, shoe, jacket, pig, cow

26. 'Preface' is to 'Book' as 'Overture' is to music, play, opera, composer, symphony

27. 'South' is to 'Direction' as 'Yellow' is to lemon, bitter, colour, sharp, rainbow

28. 'Calm' is to 'Agitated' as 'Generous' is to rich, happy, mean, poor, careless

29. 'Bicycle' is to 'Pedalo' as 'Car' is to glider, submarine, rowing boat, yacht, motor boat

30. 'Treasure' is to 'Museum' as 'Book' is to shelf, shop, stand, newsagents, library

Verbal Checking

Read through the following lists, circling any errors in the list
on the right:

1.	The Grove Studio	1.	The Grove Studio
2.	Kaleidoscope	2.	Kaliedoscope
3.	Barham's Bakery	3.	Bareham's Bakery
4.	Catlow's Farm	4.	Catlow's Farm
5.	Firm and Fresh	5.	Firm and Fressh
6.	Schugardts	6.	Schugarts
7.	The Paper Shop	7.	Paper Shop
8.	Heaven Scent	8.	Heven Sent
9.	B & J Car Repairs	9.	B & J Car Repairs
10.	Cromwell Cars	10.	Cromwell's Cars

11.	Melissa's	11.	Melisas's
12.	T. J. Hooley	12.	T. J. Hooley
13.	Harvey's Hair	13.	Harvey's Hare
14.	Thomson & Co.	14.	Thompson & Co.
15.	W. W. Wilson	15.	W. W. Wilson
16.	Babytime	16.	Babylime
17.	Ruislip's Hi-Fi	17.	Riuslips Hi-Fi
18.	Curl Up and Dye	18.	Curl Up and Die
19.	I. C. Missen	19.	I. G. Missen
20.	Haven Health	20.	Heaven Health

Tip

Comparing columns of printed information – whether of shops in a town, goods in stock or whatever – and then spotting errors seems very easy, unless you are correcting lengthy lists, and at speed. Unfortunately, that is what you will have to do in the test! To do well, you need to go as slowly as possible, concentrating fully on one line at a time. Again, be aware that some lines will have one mistake, others perhaps two or three and a few none at all. This type of work really needs to be looked at twice with a few minutes' break in-between. You will be surprised how many other errors you pick up second time around.

Below is a handwritten list of titles to be included in the 'further reading' section of a book. Check the typed list that follows, and ring any errors.

Hodgson P. and J. Effective Meetings. London, Century Business, 1992.

Martin D. Manipulating Meetings. London, Pitman in association with the Institute of Management, 1994.

Sharman D. The Perfect Meeting. London, Century Business, 1993.

Hodgson P.J. Effective Meetings. London, Century Business, 1992.

Martin P. Manipulating Meetings. London, Pitman in asociation with the Institution of Management, 1994.

Sharman D. The Perfect Meeting. London, Century Busines, 1993.

Tip

Studying handwritten text and typed copy is a popular alternative where verbal checking is concerned. As before, it needs to be tackled carefully, one line after another. Ideally, it should be looked at twice to spot any mistakes missed first time around. Always compare the second piece of copy with the first as it is the second one that contains the errors – and mark the mistakes on the second one.

Check the original data with the computer printout that follows, circling any errors on the second set of data.

Janet Strange
12 Thomas Avenue
Trimley
IP37 3NG

Marie Reynolds
76a Ranleigh Road
Dewsbury
NO31 2PF

Tracey Jones
38 Brightwell Close
Riddleswick
PA2 7DD

Lyn di Carlo
32 North Street
Dewsbury
NO31 4ZZ

Angela Ramsden
66 High Road
Downtown
GE7 3FF

Dawn Fox
43 Dawson Drive
Danwick
S13 4PM

Cathy Newby
22b High Road
Walton St Mary
IP16 OYS

Yvonne Welch
74 Acacia Avenue
Riddleswick
PA2 8MD

Janet Strange
12 Thomes Avenue
Timley
IP37 3NG

Maria Reynolds
76 Ranleigh Road
Dewbury
NO31 2PF

Tracy Jones
38 Brightwell Close
Riddleswick
DA2 7PP

Lyndi Carlo
32 North Street
Dewbsury
NO31 4SS

Angela Ramden
99 High Road
Dowtown
GE7 3FF

Dawn Fox   missed
Danwich   line
S13 4PM

Cathy Newbury
22d High Road
Walton St Mary
IP16 OYS

Yvonne Welch
74 Accacia Avenue
Ridlleswick
PA2 8MP

Tip

Two sets of well spaced out, typed copy may be included in some tests, and it is difficult to compare materials which are some pages apart and cannot be studied alongside each other. The most sensible advice here is to check, check and check again, and pay attention to detail. In this example, that means double-checking the exact spelling of names, and paying particular attention to postcodes as most errors will be contained in these.

Another Tip

Typically, many of the words that arise in verbal ability tests will be those that are both difficult to spell and are used regularly in the course of the job to which you are applying. As examples, a typist in a motoring organization might be expected to spell the names of car parts properly, whilst a doctor's receptionist would need to be able to spell medical words correctly. If you expect to face verbal ability questions of any kind, try to obtain a specialist dictionary or trade journals relevant to the industry to which you are applying. Then study them carefully.

Summary

1. Verbal ability questions are concerned with words and are designed to measure a candidate's aptitude for verbal concepts and ideas.

2. Questions relating to verbal ability can be found in a general intelligence test. Typically, they will involve:
   a. finding a missing word
   b. identifying the odd word out.

3. Verbal ability questions may also feature in a specific aptitude test. These questions might focus on:
   a. spelling
   b. word meanings
   c. verbal checking.

3

Non-verbal
Ability
Questions

Questions of this type incorporate symbols, and your responses will enable the organization to judge your ability to think in an abstract manner. Non-verbal ability questions will be seen most often in general intelligence tests.

Characteristics

Non-verbal ability questions can be diverse in nature, although the majority of them will feature one of three key themes: matching two symbols out of a choice of perhaps five or six; spotting the odd symbol from amongst five or six other ones; and continuing a series of symbols, adding one more to a row of possibly half a dozen. Examples of these are set out in this chapter, with the answers included in chapter 6. It is up to you to decide whether to approach these questions as a test or as research material. Whatever you do, check out the accompanying tips as well.

The most sensible method of preparing for non-verbal ability questions is to work through as many as you can, be aware of any tactical tips and then contemplate the answers in order to evaluate your performance. The examples in this chapter are classified under these broad headings:

- matching symbols
- spotting the odd symbol out
- continuing a series of symbols.

Matching Symbols

Identify the matching symbols by circling the appropriate letter. As an example:

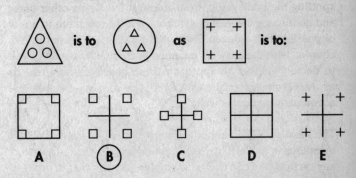

A **B** **C** **D** **E**

(The answer is **B** because the internal symbols have to become the outer one whilst that transfers into the inner ones.)

1.

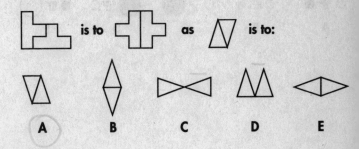

A **B** **C** **D** **E**

2.

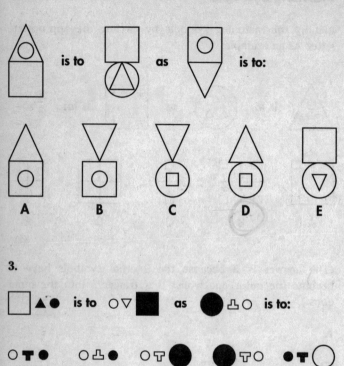

3.

4.

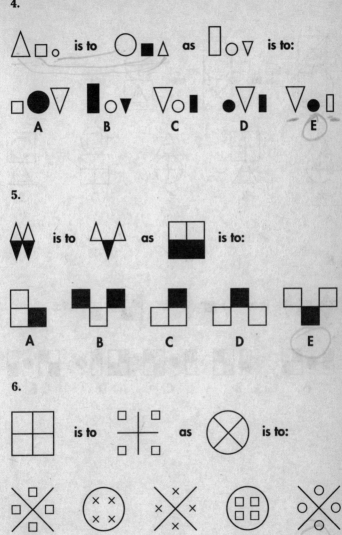

5.

6.

7.

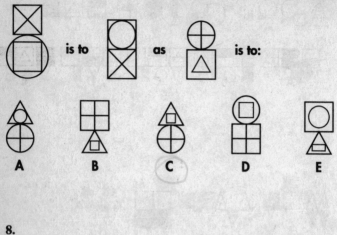

A   B   C   D   E

8.

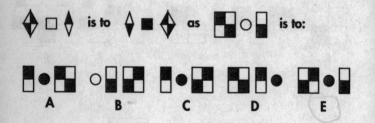

A   B   C   D   E

9.

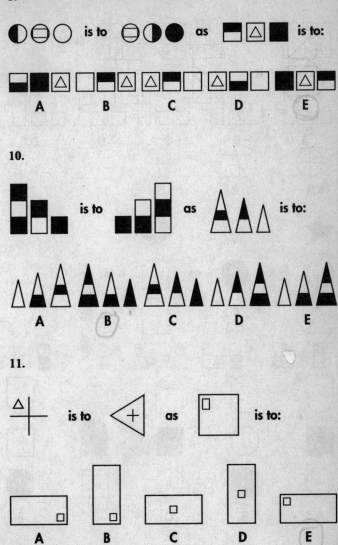

10.

11.

12.

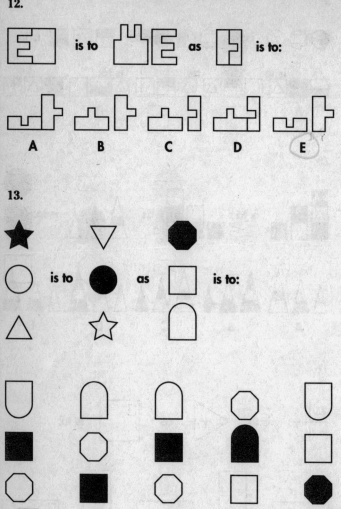

13.

60

14.

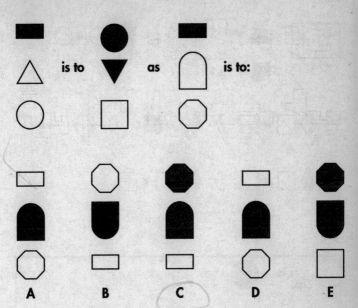

15.

Tip

The secret of success here is to stay calm and think logically. Work out how the first group of symbols became the second before looking at the third and trying to calculate which of the multiple-choice groups matches it. With question 1, for example, the symbol on the left (⊟) has moved to the right and the one there (⊔) has gone across to the left and stood up (⊟). Now apply this same sequence to the third group of symbols, and find its match. Be aware that questions like this invariably involve symbols simply (a) swapping places, (b) turning around and/or (c) changing colour. Crack the code, then you will know the right answer.

Spotting the Odd Symbol Out

Identify the odd one out by underlining the letter beneath it.

For example:

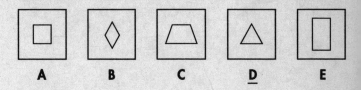

(The answer is **D** because this symbol has three sides, whereas the others have four.)

1.

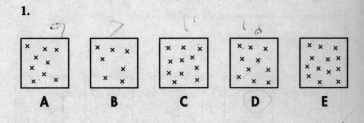

2.

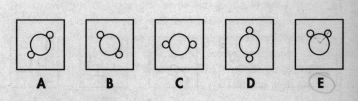

3.

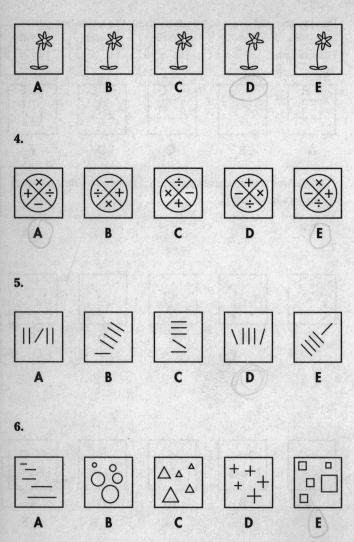

A B C D E

4.

A B C D E

5.

A B C D E

6.

A B C D E

64

7.

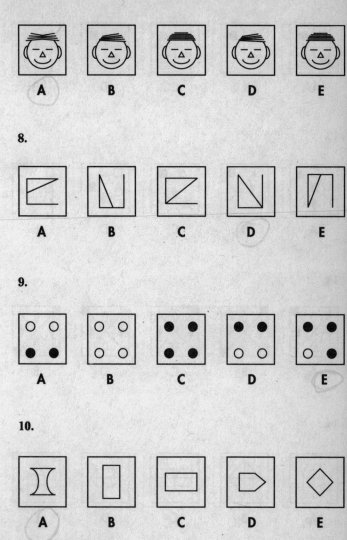

A   B   C   D   E

8.

A   B   C   D   E

9.

A   B   C   D   E

10.

A   B   C   D   E

11.

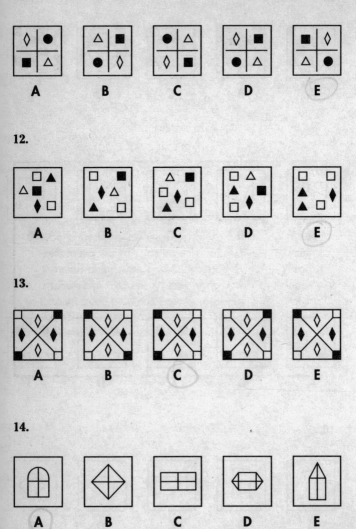

A   B   C   D   E

12.

A   B   C   D   E

13.

A   B   C   D   E

14.

A   B   C   D   E

15.

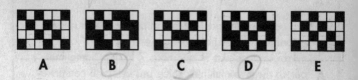

A   B   C   D   E

Tip

In many questions of this type, the odd symbol out will be distinguished by (a) an even rather than an odd number of parts (or vice versa); (b) an alternative position; (c) an extra or missing part; (d) a different sequence of parts or (e) varying sizes, as in questions 1 to 6. With these questions, it can be a good idea to take two symbols at a time, identify their similarities and then see if others share them, or not. The one that does not should be the odd one out.

Continuing a Series of Symbols

Identify the symbol that continues the sequence by circling the letter below it.

As an example:

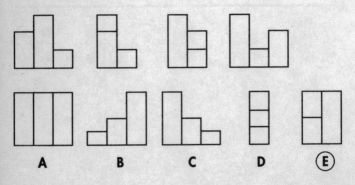

A   B   C   D   (E)

68

(The answer is **E** because the first column has moved across from left to right, then the second [now the first] column does the same, and so on.)

1.

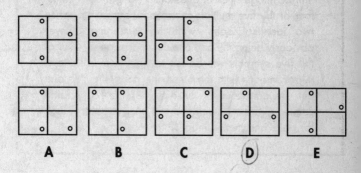

2.

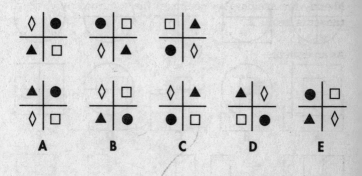

3.

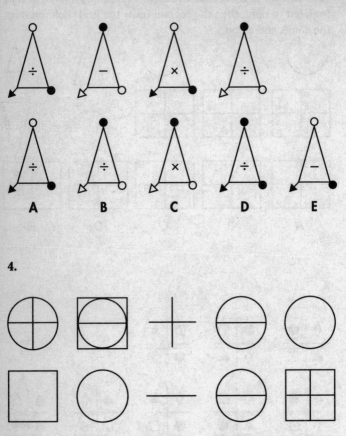

4.

5.

6.

71

7.

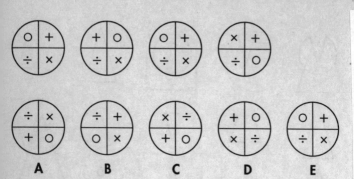

8.

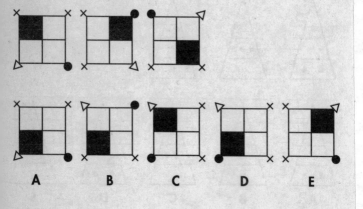

9.

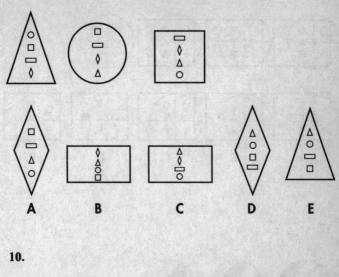

A   B   C   D   E

10.

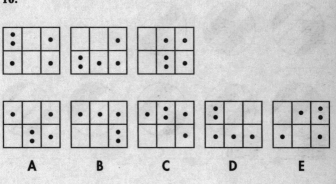

A   B   C   D   E

11.

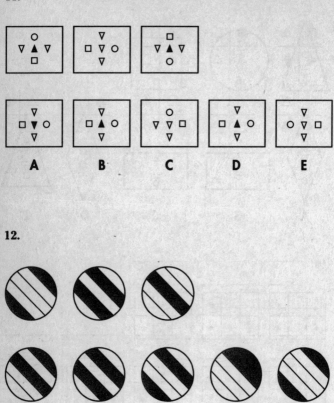

12.

13.

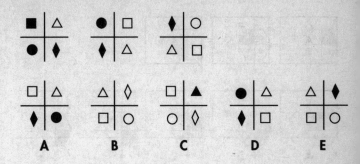

14.

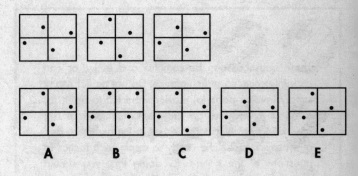

15.

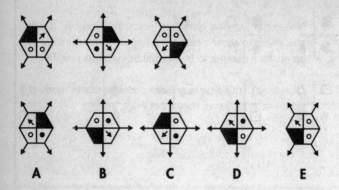

A   B   C   D   E

Tip

These questions can be complex and tricky, or can certainly seem so at first glance. Do not panic! Many simply involve parts (a) moving from left to right; (b) rotating clockwise or anti-clockwise and/or (c) alternating or fitting together, as in the example, and questions 1 to 15. Be ready to apply such tactics to questions of this nature. By doing this, you should almost certainly be able to identify the correct answer.

Summary

1. Non-verbal ability questions include symbols. Their purpose is to allow a candidate's aptitude for thinking in an abstract manner to be evaluated, as far as possible.

2. Questions of this type vary quite considerably in terms of complexity. However, they most often involve
   a. matching symbols
   b. spotting the odd symbol out
   c. continuing a series of symbols.

4

Numerical
Ability
Questions

These questions are designed to show how well you reason with numbers. Numerical ability questions feature prominently in general intelligence tests and often in specific aptitude tests too. You should have a basic understanding of the characteristics of these questions prior to working through the examples and answers that follow.

Characteristics

In general intelligence tests, questions relating to numerical ability are likely to involve adding, subtracting, multiplying, dividing, fractions, percentages and continuing a series of numbers in a logical manner. With regard to specific aptitude tests, numerical ability questions will concentrate on areas such as numerical awareness, estimation and checking. Various examples of different types of numerical ability questions are set out in this chapter. These, and their associated tips, can be studied at your leisure, or tackled as a test, whichever you prefer. To complete your understanding, check the answers in Chapter 6.

Probably the most sensible way of preparing for numerical ability questions is to go through as many as possible, contemplating the suggested tactical tips and comparing your responses to the correct answers to appraise your performance and what you did wrong.

The examples given are set out beneath these headings:

- adding and subtracting
- multiplying and dividing
- fractions and percentages
- continuing a series of numbers
- numerical awareness
- numerical estimation
- numerical checking.

Adding and Subtracting

Without using a calculator or rough paper, do the following calculations:

1. 497 + 303 + 205 =
2. 751 + 258 + 326 =
3. 97 + 36 + 12 =
4. 145 + 66 + 67 =
5. 973 + 28 + 44 =
6. 63 + 82 + 91 =
7. 16 + 133 + 12 =
8. 50 + 375 + 56 =
9. 65 + 365 + 325 =
10. 42 + 93 + 27 =

Tip

Some of these calculations will be very easy (e.g. 12 + 19), others fairly tough (e.g. 174 + 149 + 316 + 134 + 191), with the majority somewhere in-between. Whatever they are like, you will have to tackle a large number of them at great speed in a short time. As rough checks on your accuracy, you can either approximate the numbers and add them together (500 + 300 + 200 gives an idea of what 497 + 303 + 205 will be) and/or add up the last digits of each one (7 + 3 + 5 shows that 497 + 303 + 205 will end with 5).

---

11. 9564 – 3427 – 1733 =

12. 39800 – 2636 – 2534 =

13. 7027 – 3072 – 773 =

14. 63903 – 372 – 526 =

15. 3614 – 234 – 436 =

16. 27337 – 219 – 927 =

17. 5372 – 377 – 413 =

18. 48000 – 979 – 326 =

19. 3333 – 335 – 631 =

20. 92426 – 2436 – 737 =

Tip

Again, some calculations will be relatively easy, others very difficult, with most of them between these two extremes. If you have time, it is sensible to double-check your answers by subtracting rounded up or down numbers from each other.

---

21. 698 – 169 + 357 =

22. 723 + 36 – 431 =

23. 47 – 38 + 264 =

24. 299 + 374 – 287 =

25. 431 + 472 – 536 =

26. 99 + 99 – 178 =

27. $345 - 254 + 97 =$

28. $44 + 183 - 217 =$

29. $888 - 767 + 42 =$

30. $939 - 858 + 767 =$

31. $237 - 109 + 911 =$

32. $321 + 27 - 236 =$

33. $299 - 98 + 759 =$

34. $103 + 386 - 394 =$

35. $207 + 44 - 157 =$

36. $979 + 63 - 797 =$

37. $565 - 69 + 253 =$

38. $456 - 18 + 137 =$

39. $362 - 27 + 141 =$

40. $197 + 212 - 296 =$

41. $489 - 398 + 311 =$

42. $569 + 496 - 827 =$

43. $423 - 234 + 321 =$

44. $198 + 95 - 109 =$

45. $721 + 127 - 325 =$

46. $138 + 101 - 97 =$

47. $211 - 112 + 121 =$

48. $333 - 213 + 231 =$

49. $616 + 88 - 79 =$

50. $409 - 211 + 17 =$

Multiplying and Dividing

Without the aid of a calculator, do these calculations:

1. $572 \times 9 =$

2. $4626 \times 17 =$

3. $66813 \times 4 =$

4. $712 \times 5 =$

5. $773 \times 0 =$

6. $4111 \times 11 =$

7. $1731 \times 102 =$

8. $462 \times 41 =$

9. $323 \times 33 =$

10. $610 \times 10 =$

11. $4128 \div 96 =$

12. $6237 \div 81 =$

13. $7623 \div 77 =$

14. $3196 \div 47 =$

15. $6048 \div 27 =$

16. $1558 \div 19 =$

17. $861 \div 41 =$

18. $1558 \div 19 =$

19. $1095 \div 73 =$

20. $315 \div 45 =$

21. $18 \times 4 \div 9 =$

22. $17 \times 32 \div 16 =$

23. $993 \div 3 \times 10 =$

24. $105 \div 7 \times 45 =$

25. $324 \div 36 \times 9 =$

26. $70 \times 5 \div 14 =$

27. $66 \times 30 \div 33 =$

28. $11 \times 110 \div 22 =$

29. $16 \times 152 \div 8 =$

30. $12 \div 0 \times 3 =$

31. $17 \times 8 \div 4 =$

32. $14 \div 2 \times 21 =$

33. $61 \times 12 \div 4 =$

34. $32 \div 4 \times 11 =$

35. $88 \div 11 \times 32 =$

36. $19 \times 14 \div 38 =$

37. $15 \times 5 \div 25 =$

38. $7 \times 80 \div 4 =$

39. $44 \times 11 \div 4 =$

40. $16 \div 2 \times 9 =$

41. $23 \times 15 \div 3 =$

42. $37 \times 9 \div 3 =$

43. $42 \div 2 \times 11 =$

44. $96 \div 3 \times 14 =$

45. $99 \times 2 \div 6 =$

46. $95 \div 5 \times 19 =$

47. $13 \times 32 \div 4 =$

48. $11 \times 22 \div 2 =$

49. $28 \div 4 \times 9 =$

50. $47 \times 15 \div 5 =$

Fractions and Percentages

Attempt these calculations:

1. $\frac{3}{3} =$

2. $\frac{20}{2} =$

3. $\frac{12}{4} =$

4. $\frac{60}{?} = 12$

5. $\frac{72}{?} = 4$

6. $\frac{?}{2} = 3$

7. $\frac{?}{3} = 9$

8. $\frac{1}{3} + \frac{2}{6} + \frac{1}{4} =$

9. $\frac{2}{5} + \frac{3}{4} + \frac{1}{2} =$

10. $\frac{3}{5} - \frac{1}{2}$ =

11. $\frac{4}{6} + \frac{3}{4}$ =

12. $6 \times \frac{3}{5}$ =

13. $8 \times \frac{1}{3}$ =

14. ✗ $9 \div \frac{2}{3}$ = $13\frac{1}{v}$.

15. $12 \div \frac{1}{4}$ =

16. $\frac{2}{3}$ of 63 =

17. $\frac{1}{9}$ of 27 =

18. $\frac{4}{5}$ of 100 =

19. $\frac{3}{4}$ of 80 =

20. $\frac{1}{3}$ of 96 =

Tip

Fractions really test your multiplying and dividing skills. To calculate the missing number from a fraction like $\frac{A}{B}$ = C, you can do any of these, as appropriate: A ÷ B = C, A ÷ C = B, B × C = A. Try them on questions 1 to 7. They work! To add or subtract fractions, find the lowest possible number which all the 'B's can be multiplied into. For $\frac{1}{2} + \frac{4}{5}$ it would be 10 ($\underline{2} \times 5 = 10$, $\underline{5} \times 2 = 10$). Then multiply the 'A's by the same amounts ($\underline{1} \times 5 = 5$, $\underline{4} \times 2 = 8$) to reach fractions which can be added or subtracted easily ($\frac{5}{10} + \frac{8}{10} = \frac{13}{10}$) and a final number reached ($\frac{3}{10} = 1\frac{13}{10}$). Apply these to questions 8 to 11.

Another Tip

When multiplying a whole number (10) by a fraction
($\frac{2}{3}$), just multiply the number by 'A' and put it onto 'B'
(10 × 2 = 20, $\frac{20}{3} = 6\frac{2}{3}$). If dividing, do exactly the
same (10 ÷ $\frac{1}{5}$ = 10 x 1 = 10, $\frac{10}{5}$ = 2). Have a go at
questions 12 to 15. To find a fraction of a whole
number ($\frac{3}{7}$ of 140), divide the whole number by 'B'
and multiply by 'A' (140 ÷ 7 = 20, 20 x 3 = 60). Look
at questions 16 to 20.

21.   25% of 60 =

22.   32% of 100 =

23.   65% of 3000 =

24.   16% of 450 =

25.   31% of ? = 279

26.   5% of ? = 7

27.   12% of ? = 6

28.   ? of 80 = 24

29.   ? of 32 = 8

30.   ? of 1000 = 770

31. 50% of 78 =

32. 12% of 2000 =

33. 15% of 680 =

34. 2% of 3600 =

35. 9% of 5000 =

36. 4% of 9000 =

37. 87% of 300 =

38. 60% of 350 =

39. 92% of ? = 276

40. 36% of ? = 432

41. 91% of ? = 819

42. 5% of ? = 30

43. 18% of ? = 81

44. 19% of ? = 171

45. ? % of 750 = 225

46. ? % of 120 = 18

47. ? % of 36 = 18

48. ? % of 88 = 22

49. ? % of 140 = 56

50. ? % of 840 = 168

Tip

Like fractions, percentages test your multiplying and dividing skills. To find a percentage (30%) of a number (90), divide the number by 100 and multiply it by the percentage (90 ÷ 100 × 30 = 27). Test this out on questions 21 to 24 and 31 to 38. To discover the missing number (17% of ? = 85), reverse the process, dividing the resulting figure by the percentage and multiplying by 100 (85 ÷ 17 × 100 = 500). Take a look at questions 25 to 27 and 39 to 44 to confirm this tactic works in practice. To calculate the missing percentage (?% of 60 = 12), multiply the resulting figure by 100 and divide by the number (12 × 100 ÷ 60 = 20%). Use this on questions 28 to 30 and 45 to 50.

Continuing a Series of Numbers

Identify the reasoning behind the following series of numbers and complete the sequence.

As an example:

29, 23, 18, 14, 11, 9 ____

29, 23, 18, 14, 11, 9, 8 (-6, -5, -4, -3, -2, -1)

1. 16, 4, 8, 2, 4, 1, ____

2. 17, 14, 20, 17, 23, 20, ____

3. 10, 12, 13, 15, 16, 18, ____

4. 22, 17, 24, 19, 26, 21, ____

5. 1, 8, 22, 43, 71, 106, ____

6. 12, 15, 11, 14, 10, 13, ____

7. 0, 1, 3, 4, 6, 7, ____

8. 10, 10, 12, 12, 14, 14, ____

9. 1, 4, 10, 19, 31, 46, ____

10. 1, 3, 6, 10, 15, 21, ____

11. 1, 1, 2, 6, 24, 120, ____

12. 10, 5, 6, 3, 4, 2, ____

13. 1, 4, 9, 16, 25, 36, ____

14. 0, 10, 10, 20, 30, 50, ____

15. 2, 5, 12, 27, 58, 121, ____

16. 8, 9, 11, 14, 18, 23, ____

17. 23, 22, 11, 10, 5, 4, ____

18. 12, 16, 18, 22, 24, 28, ____

19. 21, 7, 12, 4, 9, 3, ____

20. 10, 9, 11, 8, 12, 7, ____

21. 19, 20, 23, 28, 35, 44, ____

22. 6, 3, 9, 6, 18, 15, ____

23. 9, 6, 12, 9, 15, 12, ____

24. 11, 6, 10, 7, 9, 8, ____

25. 8, 4, 12, 6, 18, 9, ____

26. 5, 10, 11, 22, 23, 46, ____

27. 0, 2, 2, 4, 6, 10, ____

28. 1, 3, 8, 19, 42, 89, ____

29. 3, 3, 6, 9, 15, 24, ____

30. 10, 28, 82, 244, 730, 2188, ____

Tip

Most sequences are easy to recognize or can be identified promptly by mixing +, −, ×, together. Start with the first two numbers and spot possible links, then work through the other numbers in turn to see which link is applicable to all. A few sequences will add adjacent numbers together to get to the next one, as in question 14, so watch out for this. Some may be more complicated with 'double calculations' needing to be made (× and + or ÷ and −), as in question 15. Be careful of these as well.

Numerical Awareness

In these questions, you have to find and correct errors in calculating totals. Draw a line through any errors, writing the correct amounts alongside them.

1. 'Babytime'

1 'Sleepy Dreams' Cot	@	£149.95	£149.95
2 'Teddies' Bumpers	@	£35.99	£70.98
1 Cot Mattress	@	£45.00	£45.00
1 Cot Pillow	@	£3.99	£3.99
3 Stretch Sheets	@	£2.95	£8.85
3 Pillow Cases	@	£1.99	£5.97
2 Valances	@	£3.95	£7.99
1 Teddy Bear	@	£12.99	£12.99
		Total	**£305.27**

2. 'Royal Oak'

2 Chilli Con Carne	@	£4.95	£9.90
1 Lasagne	@	£4.50	£4.50
2 Mixed Grills	@	£3.75	£7.50
1 House Red	@	£6.95	£6.95
1 House White	@	£6.95	£8.95
3 Black Forest Gâteaus	@	£1.75	£4.25
1 Apple Pie	@	£1.50	£1.50
1 Chocolate Mousse	@	£1.99	£1.99
3 Coffees	@	£0.70	£2.80
2 Teas	@	£0.60	£1.20
Subtotal			£47.58
Service Charge @ 10%			£ 4.76
		Total	**£52.34**

3. 'Furniture World'

1 × 'Nathaniel' Dining Room Table	@	£339.95	£339.95
2 × 'Nathaniel' Carver Chairs	@	£99.95	£199.90
4 × 'Nathaniel' Dining Room Chairs	@	£79.99	£391.96
1 × 'Gayfer' Wall Unit	@	£799.99	£799.95
1 × 'Riseborough' CD Storage Unit	@	£46.25	£46.25
1 × 'Diana' Recliner (Green)	@	£235.65	£265.65
2 × Armchair Protectors	@	£3.99	£7.98
1 × Footstool	@	£19.95	£19.99
		Subtotal	£2071.63
	Discount @ 10%		£207.16
		Total	**£1864.47**

4. 'R & J Spares'

Quantity	Part Number	Unit Cost	Total
2	AJX–3130	£2.99	£5.98
3	AJX–3100	£3.95	£7.90
2	AJX–3912	£4.90	£9.80
3	BCM–4213	£2.95	£8.85
1	BCM–4312	£3.99	£3.99
5	NDR–2610	£2.95	£14.75
2	NDR–2595	£2.99	£5.98
3	AJX–3170	£4.99	£9.98
3	AJX–3175	£4.95	£14.75
2	AJX–3182	£4.95	£10.90
		Subtotal	£92.88
	VAT @ 17.5%		£16.25
		Total	**£109.13**

5. 'Hollis Consultancy Services'

Date	Hours	Hourly Rate	Expenses	Total
15/4	4 (pm)	£24.95	–	£99.80
17/4	7 (am/pm)	£24.95	£15.00	£189.65
19/4	4 (am)	£24.95	–	£99.80
22/4	4 (pm)	£24.95	£12.95	£112.75
24/4	7 (am/pm)	£24.95	£15.00	£189.65
26/4	4 (am)	£24.95	–	£99.80
29/4	4 (pm)	£24.95	£12.95	£112.75
1/5	7 (am/pm)	£24.95	£15.00	£189.65
3/5	4 (pm)	£24.95	–	£99.80
			Total	**£1193.55**

Tip

Attention to detail is the key to success here. Check and double-check each line (or column) in turn. Be especially wary when you spot a major, obvious mistake – there is often a minor, easy-to-overlook one hiding alongside or next to it. Also, look closely at subtotals, remembering to amend them if earlier figures have proved to be incorrect. It is easy to forget to do this, and many candidates do!

Numerical Estimation

With these questions, you have to give estimated answers to complicated calculations. Each calculation is too hard to do quickly in your head and there is not enough time to work it out on paper. Therefore, you must indicate an approximate answer by putting lines through the two adjacent boxes which represent those sums closest to the actual answer.

1. An author writes 2750 words per day and works a four-and-a-half day week. How many weeks would it take to complete an 85,000-word book?

    5 weeks   ☐

    6 weeks   ☐

    7 weeks   ☐

    8 weeks   ☐

    9 weeks   ☐

    10 weeks   ☐

2. A car averages $8\frac{3}{4}$ miles to one litre. Over the next week, it will be used for six journeys of 221 miles, 108 miles, 323 miles, 77 miles, 103 miles and 189 miles. How many litres of petrol will it use in total?

    90 litres   ☐

    100 litres   ☐

    110 litres   ☐

    120 litres   ☐

    130 litres   ☐

    140 litres   ☐

3. A teacher has 33 pupils in a class and sets each of them an essay to write for homework. It takes 12 minutes to mark an essay. How long would it take the teacher to mark all the pupils' homework?

4 hours ☐

5 hours ☐

6 hours ☐

7 hours ☐

8 hours ☐

9 hours ☐

10 hours ☐

4. A window cleaner averages three houses an hour, at £2.50 each, and works a seven-hour day, five days per week. What is the window cleaner's weekly income?

£175 ☐

£200 ☐

£225 ☐

£250 ☐

£275 ☐

£300 ☐

5. A salesperson drives on average 137 miles each day, five days per week. After how many weeks' driving would the car's 5,000-mile service need to be carried out?

5 weeks ☐

6 weeks ☐

7 weeks ☐

8 weeks ☐

9 weeks ☐

10 weeks ☐

Tip

Nine times out of ten, you can round all numbers up and down to simplify your calculations, and your answer will still be accurate enough to be correct. Try it with the questions above. However, the success of this tactic does depend on how many possible responses are listed and how broad they are. The more there are, the more precise your calculation must be.

Numerical Checking

Here, you have to find errors in various tables of numbers. Put a circle around any errors that you see.

1.

Index	Sex	Age	Status	Index	Sex	Age	Status
00360	1	34	13/27	00360	1	34	13/27
00731	2	31	12/16	00731	2	31	12/16
00636	1	21	12/16	00366	1	21	12/16
01717	2	27	3/08	00717	2	26	3/08
00421	1	31	3/08	00421	1	31	3/08
00391	1	19	3/08	00391	1	19	13/08
10246	1	51	15/30	01246	1	41	15/30
00355	2	41	15/30	00335	2	51	15/30
00261	1	30	13/27	00261	1	30	15/30
01271	1	29	13/27	01271	1	29	13/27

2.

	Oct	Nov	Dec	Jan	Feb	Mar
Income	2,000	2,300	1,700	2,300	2,000	1,700
Expenditure	1,800	1,200	2,000	1,800	1,200	2,000
Balance	200	1,100	–300	500	800	–300
Opening Bk. Bal.	500	700	1,800	1,500	2,000	2,800
Closing Bk. Bal.	700	1,800	1,500	2,000	2,800	2,500

	Oct	Nov	Dec	Jan	Feb	Mar
Income	2,000	2,300	1,700	2,300	2,000	1,700
Expenditure	1,800	1,200	2,000	1,800	1,200	2,000
Balance	200	1,100	–300	500	600	–300
Opening Bk. Bal.	500	700	1,800	1,500	2,000	2,800
Closing Bk. Bal.	700	1,800	1,700	2,000	2,800	2,300

3.

a.	46714	37610	32416
b.	46124	43123	47111
c.	41331	42164	49130
d.	37101	39121	34576
e.	33192	31912	39113
f.	42224	41136	43411
g.	51000	51603	58734
h.	43621	43266	44943
i.	33333	31733	43917
j.	26363	27319	24318
k.	33639	33991	38410
l.	44814	48148	44418

a.	36714	37610	32416
b.	46124	43123	47111
c.	41331	42164	49130
d.	37101	39121	34576
e.	33192	39211	39113
f.	42224	41316	43411
g.	51000	51603	58734
h.	43621	43226	44943
i.	33333	31773	34917
j.	26363	27319	24318
k.	33639	33911	38410
l.	44814	48418	44418

4.

	Apr	May	Jun	Jul	Aug	Sep
BAKER C.	37,132	39,246	30,003	31,414	39,414	42,413
MOFFAT P.	26,319	29,318	26,434	30,777	29,646	32,133
BENTINE M.	40,010	41,326	34,137	30,324	39,261	39,310
DALE J.	37,200	38,420	36,220	36,315	32,717	39,216
PERTWEE J.	50,200	38,701	43,620	44,445	45,424	38,381
CUSACK P.	24,190	24,004	26,270	29,312	31,311	28,711

	Apr	May	Jun	Jul	Aug	Sep
BAKER C.	37,132	39,246	30,003	31,626	39,414	42,413
MOFFAT P.	26,319	29,318	26,434	30,777	29,646	32,133
BENTINE M.	40,010	41,326	34,137	30,324	39,261	39,310
DALE J.	37,212	38,420	36,220	36,315	32,717	39,216
PERTWEE J.	50,200	38,701	43,230	44,455	45,424	38,321
CUSACK P.	24,190	24,004	26,270	29,321	31,331	28,711

5.

1.	27–1350	31–3160	31–3130	32–1360
2.	19–7217	14–7211	12–3106	19–4210
3.	18–1717	19–1171	13–1177	14–1777
4.	19–2641	23–9210	43–6121	22–6100
5.	21–6666	71–9426	16–6666	11–2121
6.	31–3103	18–6141	21–9213	18–4341
7.	27–9207	17–4222	33–4133	17–2882
8.	19–4164	13–7100	27–1200	19–9119
9.	18–8321	12–9210	41–9200	81–1818
10.	14–2381	13–1000	14–3369	77–1777

1.	27–1350	31–3160	31–3130	32–1360
2.	19–7217	14–7211	12–3016	19–4120
3.	18–7171	19–1171	13–1177	14–1177
4.	19–2641	23–9210	43–6121	22–6100
5.	31–3103	18–6141	21–9213	18–4341
6.	21–6666	71–9246	16–6666	11–2121
7.	27–9207	17–4222	33–4133	17–2882
8.	19–4164	13–7100	27–1200	19–1919
9.	18–8321	12–9210	41–9220	81–1818
10.	14–2381	13–1000	14–3369	77–7777

Tip

Check, check, and check again is the best advice for this type of question. Work down and across and do it once more to be absolutely certain (and even then you may find one or two more mistakes if you come back to it later on). Take an especially close look around any obvious errors as one or two other, minor ones tend to be located nearby, and are often overlooked by candidates concentrating hard on the major ones.

Another Tip

If you are going to face numerical aptitude questions of any kind, try to obtain and familiarize yourself with the types of documentation used in the job, whether invoices, credit and debit notes, or budgets and cash-flow forecasts. More likely than not, these will form the basis of the test questions – so be prepared!

Summary

1. Numerical ability questions focus on numbers and are employed to appraise a candidate's aptitude for reasoning with them.

2. Questions linked to numerical ability will be found in a general intelligence test. Normally, they will involve:
    a. adding and subtracting
    b. multiplying and dividing
    c. fractions and percentages
    d. continuing a series of numbers.

3. Numerical ability questions can also feature in a specific aptitude test. Such questions might concentrate on:
    a. numerical awareness
    b. numerical estimation
    c. numerical checking.

5

Spatial
Ability
Questions

Questions of this nature involve shapes. They will reveal how well you can think spatially by asking you, for example, to visualize flat shapes as solid objects and vice versa. Spatial ability questions may be found occasionally in general intelligence tests, or more extensively in specific tests if the organization requires a person with this particular aptitude. Be conscious of the characteristics of these questions before working through the numerous examples that follow, and their respective answers.

Characteristics

Spatial ability questions tend to be varied in their approach. Most of them, however, concentrate on one of three key themes: fitting shapes together, creating solid objects from flat shapes and unfolding solid objects to make flattened shapes. Examples of these are included in this chapter, with the answers in Chapter 6. You must decide how you will tackle these questions and answers: either as a test or as revision material. Whatever your choice, study carefully the associated tactical tips, which may help you to do even better when you sit the real test.

To gain the fullest possible understanding of spatial ability questions, it is probably best to look at as many as you can, take note of any accompanying tips and then appraise the answers to evaluate how well you did. The examples that follow are grouped under three, broad headings:

- fitting shapes together
- creating solid objects
- unfolding solid objects.

Fitting Shapes Together

Identify the shapes which fit together by underlining the appropriate letter. For example:

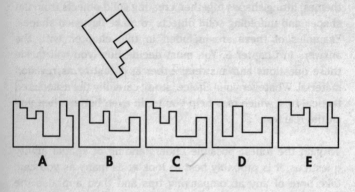

A   B   <u>C</u>   D   E

1.

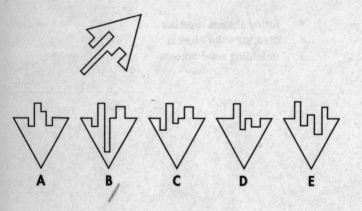

A   B   C   D   E

2.

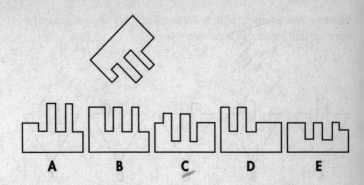

A   B   C   D   E

3.

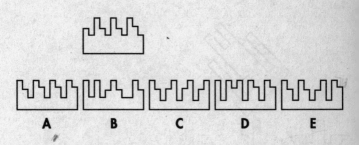

A   B   C   D   E

4.

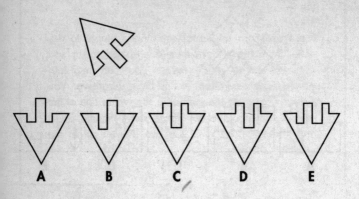

A B C D E

5.

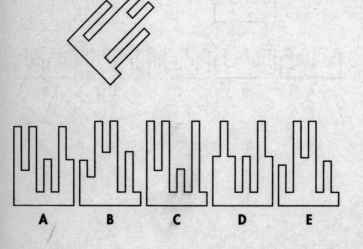

A B C D E

114

Now identify those shapes which are the same, by circling the relevant letter. As an example:

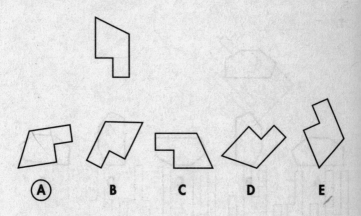

115

6.

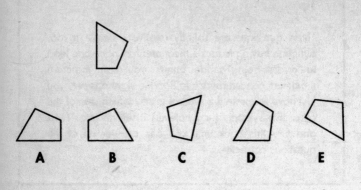

A   **B**   **C**   **D**   **E**

7.

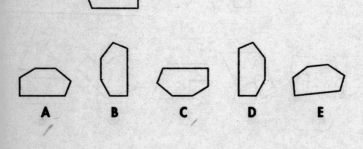

A   **B**   **C**   **D**   **E**

8.

A   B   C   D   E

9.

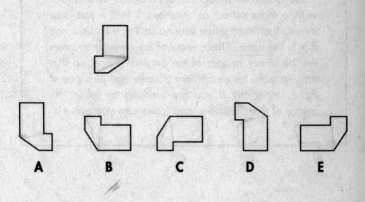

A   B   C   D   E

10.

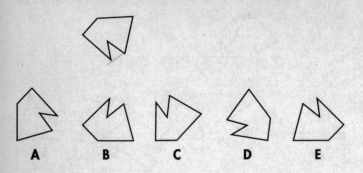

A   B   C   D   E

The following shape is made up of three of the four smaller shapes. Underline the one smaller shape which does not fit into the larger shape.

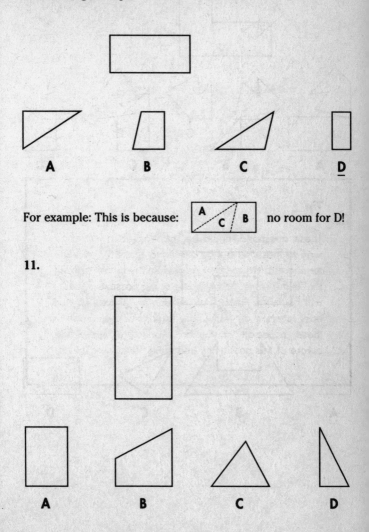

A   **B**   **C**   **D̲**

For example: This is because: no room for D!

11.

A   **B**   **C**   **D**

12.

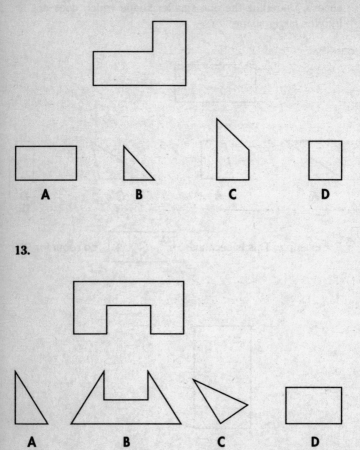

A   B   C   D

13.

A   B   C   D

14.

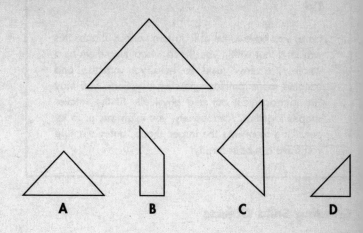

15.

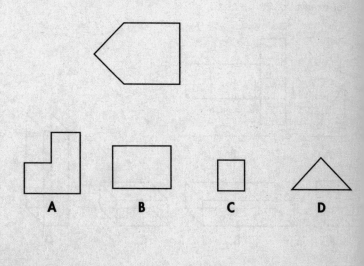

Creating Solid Objects

Identify the solid object that will be created by folding together the flat pattern, underlining the appropriate letter.

For example:

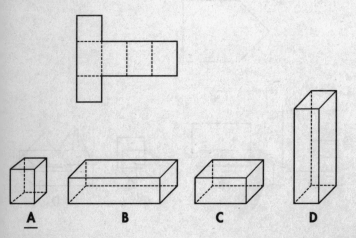

A **B** **C** **D**

122

1.

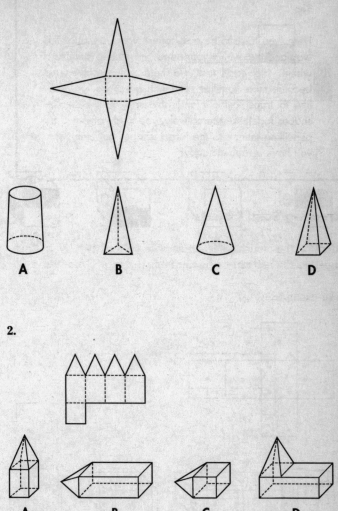

A   **B**   **C**   **D**

2.

A   **B**   **C**   **D**

3.

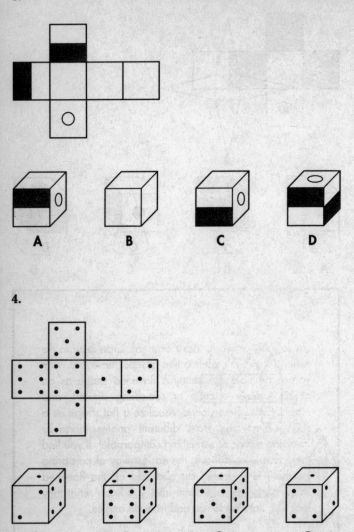

4.

124

5.

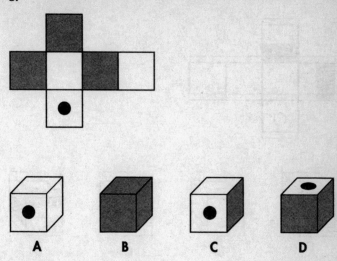

A   B   C   D

Tip

These questions look tricky until you know how to do them. Often, they fall into two groups: those that want you to be able to identify a flattened shape as an object (usually a cube or something similar), and others that require you to visualize a flat shape as a solid object and from different angles (normally involving a dice or something comparable). If you find these questions difficult, the easiest way of preparing for them is to trace, cut and fold up the flattened shapes, playing with them until you know what they look like flat, made up, and from all angles.

6.

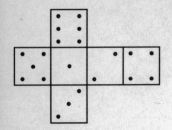

A · · · · · B · · · · C · · · · · D · · · ·

A   B   C   D

7.

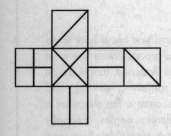

A   B   C   D

8.

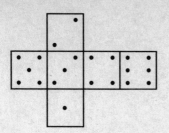

A **B** **C** **D**

9.

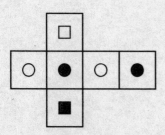

A **B** **C** **D**

10.

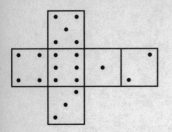

A   **B**   **C**   **D**

11.

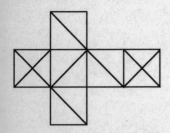

A   **B**   **C**   **D**

12.

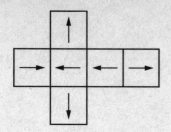

A   B   C   D

13.

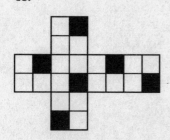

A   B   C   D

14.

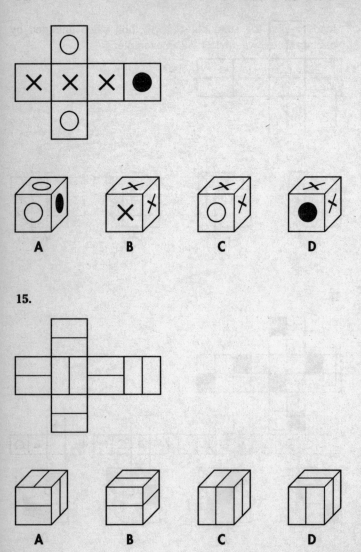

A   **B**   **C**   **D**

15.

A   **B**   **C**   **D**

130

Unfolding Solid Objects

Identify how the solid objects will look when unfolded by circling the relevant letter. As an example:

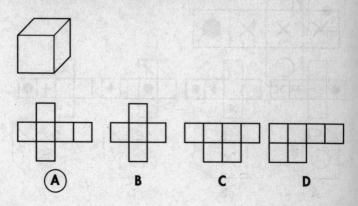

A   B   C   D

1.

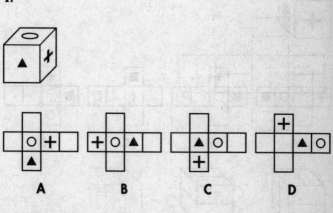

A   B   C   D

2.

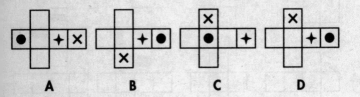

A   B   C   D

3.

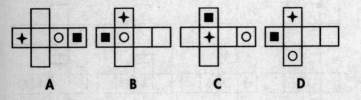

A   B   C   D

4.

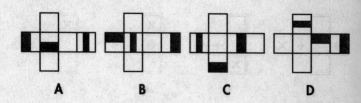

A   B   C   D

5.

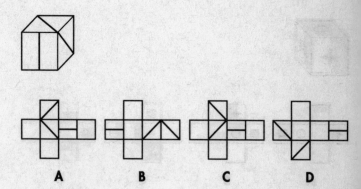

A   B   C   D

6.

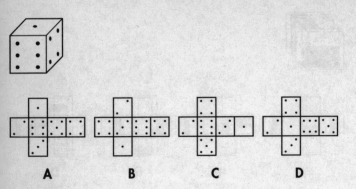

A   B   C   D

7.

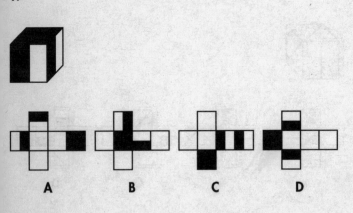

A   B   C   D

134

8.

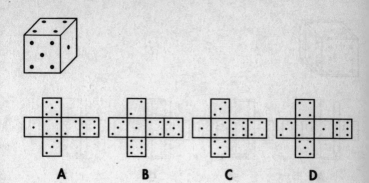

A   B   C   D

9.

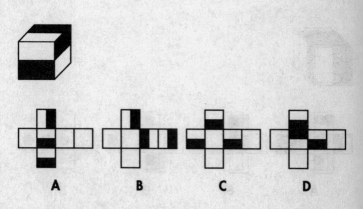

A   B   C   D

10.

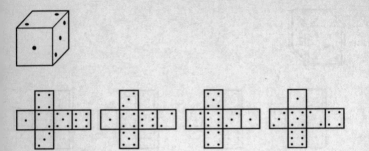

A   B   C   D

11.

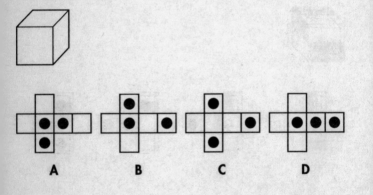

A   B   C   D

136

12.

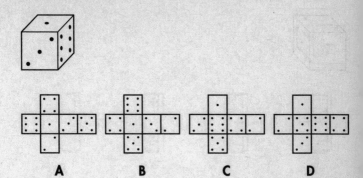

A   B   C   D

13.

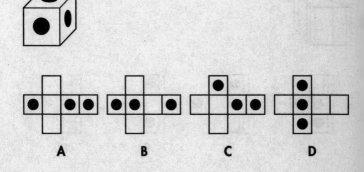

A   B   C   D

14.

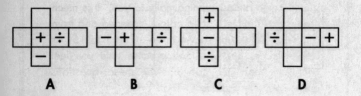

| A | B | C | D |

15.

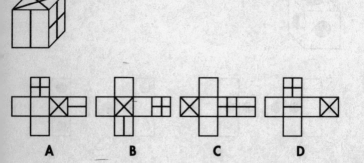

138

Tip

In many respects, these are very similar questions to the previous ones. This time, however, you need to be capable of viewing a solid object as a flat shape (if you have been practising with cut-out shapes, this should come almost automatically to you). It is much harder to visualize a solid object, flattened and from a different angle, as shown in questions 1 to 15. As before, trace, cut, fold and practise until you feel confident that you can answer these questions properly on the big day.

Summary

1. Spatial ability questions incorporate shapes. They are put into general intelligence and specific aptitude tests to enable a candidate's ability to think spatially to be appraised, as far as possible.

2. Questions of this type may be varied and diverse. Normally they involve:
    a. fitting shapes together
    b. creating solid objects
    c. unfolding solid objects.

6

The

Answers

These are the answers to the numerous verbal, non-verbal, numerical and spatial ability questions listed in Chapters 2, 3, 4 and 5. Study them, and make sure you understand the reasons for the answers. If you do not, look again at the questions and the tips that follow them until you feel confident that you can tackle them successfully should they appear in your forthcoming test. Then go and succeed at that aptitude test!

1
Verbal
Ability Answers

Finding a Missing Word

1. paper
2. flap
3. less
4. boy
5. work
6. man
7. point
8. trap
9. pen
10. week
11. land
12. pipe
13. sack
14. bath
15. saw

Identifying the Odd Word Out

1. cribbage
2. sugar
3. crab
4. bread
5. bat
6. sparrow
7. tomato
8. attack
9. joke
10. run

Spelling

1. (a) occasional
2. (c) exaggerate
3. (a) fulfil
4. (a) ceiling
5. (a) parallel
6. (a) rhythm
7. (c) disappear
8. (c) accommodate
9. (b) susceptible
10. (b) prejudice
11. (a) embarrassment
12. (c) committee
13. (b) compatible
14. (a) temporary
15. (c) consensus
16. (c) disgraceful
17. (a) preparation
18. (c) beneficial
19. (b) guaranteed
20. (c) debatable
21. vacancies
22. media

23. roofs

24. ambiguities

25. businesses

26. taxis

27. customers

28. shelves

29. stadia

30. companies

31. the office was very quite/quiet this morning.

32. I am to/too busy to do it today.

33. The noise effected/affected my concentration.

34. I put the letter threw/through the letterbox.

35. They say there/their cheque is in the post.

36. There is a draft/draught coming from that window.

37. We did not no/know that an order had been sent.

38. We will visit customers werever/wherever they are.

39. I switched of/off the computer when I finished working.

40. The local priest performed the last rites on the dying man – correct!

Word Meanings

1. erase
2. dappled
3. urbane
4. succinct
5. rest
6. poisonous
7. secret
8. vigorous
9. obscene
10. rough
11. impetuous
12. destroy
13. humility
14. refuse
15. regular
16. postscript
17. mild
18. dull
19. alienate
20. usual
21. bush
22. scissors
23. smell
24. candle
25. skin
26. opera
27. colour
28. mean
29. motor boat
30. library

Verbal Checking

1.	The Grove Studio	1.	The Grove Studio
2.	Kaleidoscope	2.	Kaliedoscope
3.	Barham's Bakery	3.	Bareham's Bakery
4.	Catlow's Farm	4.	Catlow's Farm
5.	Firm and Fresh	5.	Firm and Fressh
6.	Schugardts	6.	Schugarts
7.	The Paper Shop	7.	Paper Shop
8.	Heaven Scent	8.	Heven Sent
9.	B & J Car Repairs	9.	B & J Car Repairs
10.	Cromwell Cars	10.	Crowell's Cars
11.	Melissa's	11.	Melisa's
12.	T.J. Hooley	12.	T.J. Hooley
13.	Harvey's Hair	13.	Harvey's Hare
14.	Thomson & Co.	14.	Thompson & Co.
15.	W.W. Wilson	15.	W.W. Wilson
16.	Babytime	16.	Babytime
17.	Ruislip's Hi-Fi	17.	Ruislips Hi-Fi
18.	Curl Up and Dye	18.	Curl Up and Die
19.	I.C. Missen	19.	I.G. Missen
20.	Haven Health	20.	Heaven Health

Hodgson P. and J. Effective Meetings. London, Century Business, 1992.

Martin D. Manipulating Meetings. London, Pitman in association with the Institute of Management, 1994.

Sharman D. The Perfect Meeting. London, Century Business, 1993.

Hodgson P.J. Effective Meetings. London, Century Business, 1992.

Martin P. Manipulating Meetings. London, Pitman in association with the Institution of Management, 1994.

Sharman D. The Perfect Meeting. London, Century Business, 1993.

Janet Strange
12 Thomas Avenue
Trimley
IP37 3NG

Marie Reynolds
76a Ranleigh Road
Dewsbury
NO31 2PF

Tracey Jones
38 Brightwell Close
Riddleswick
PA2 7DD

Lyn Di Carlo
32 North Street
Dewsbury
NO31 4ZZ

Angela Ramsden
66 High Road
Downtown
GE7 3FF

Dawn Fox
43 Dawson Drive
Danwich
S13 4PM

Cathy Newby
22b High Road
Walton St Mary
IP16 OYS

Yvonne Welch
74 Acacia Avenue
Riddleswick
PA2 8MD

Janet Strange
12 Thomes Avenue
Tinley
IP37 3NG

Maria Reynolds
76 Ranleigh Road
Dewbury
NO31 2PF

Tracy Jones
38 Brightwell Close
Riddleswick
DA2 7PP

Lynda Carlo
32 North Street
Dewsbury
NO31 4SS

Angela Ramden
99 High Road
Dowtown
GE7 3FF

Dawn Fox
Danwich
S13 4PM

152

Cathy Newbury
22d High Road
Walton St Mary
IP16 0YS

Yvonne Welch
74 Acacia Avenue
Riddleswick
PA2 8MP

2

Non-verbal

Ability Answers

Matching Symbols

1. A. The symbol on the left goes to the right. The one on the right moves to the left and is raised horizontally.

2. C. The symbol at the bottom goes up. The symbol on top moves down and is turned inside out.

3. E. The symbol on the left goes to the far right, and changes colour. The one in the middle remains there but changes colour and is turned upside down. The symbol on the right comes across to the left and changes colour.

4. E. The largest symbol on the left goes to the far right and becomes the smallest. The one in the middle remains in the same size and position but changes colour. The smallest symbol on the right comes across to the left, and becomes the largest.

5. E. The two black symbols on the bottom merge into one whilst the two white ones on top separate and are supported by the single black one below.

6. E. The inner part of the symbol remains the same shape and size, and in the same position. The outside part turns into four small versions of itself which go within the inner part.

7. C. The symbol on top moves to the bottom. The symbol below turns itself inside out, and goes on top.

8. C. The symbols to the left and right swap places, and their colours are reversed. The symbol in the middle stays there, but changes colour.

9. D. The symbol on the left moves to the middle, and reverses its colours. The one in the middle goes to the left, but otherwise remains the same. The symbol on the right stays in that position, but changes its colours.

10. E. The symbols to the left and right swap positions, and their colours are reversed. The one in-between remains there, but changes its colours around.

11. C. The large symbol becomes much smaller, and remains in the same place. The same symbol turns on its side, becomes much larger and fits over the reduced symbol.

12. E. The two parts of the symbol separate. The one on the left moves to the right. The other goes to the left and turns clockwise onto its side.

13. A. The symbol on top moves to the bottom and changes colour. The one in the middle remains there but switches colour too. The symbol at the bottom goes to the top and turns upside down.

14. E. The symbol at the top goes to the bottom, changes colour and grows larger. The one in the middle stays in that position but turns upside down and changes colour as well. The symbol on the bottom goes to the top, and switches colour.

15. C. The three-part symbol on the left turns clockwise onto its side. The symbol in-between divides itself into two pieces, the left side of which changes colour. The three part symbol to the right switches proportions from small to large or vice versa, as appropriate, and reverses its colours too.

Spotting the Odd Symbol Out

1. D. It is the only one with an even number of crosses – 10.

2. E. Unlike the others, the small circles are not directly opposite each other across the large circle.

3. D. It has five petals; the others have six.

4. E. This is the only one which does not follow the ×, ÷, –, + sequence.

5. D. Unlike the other symbols, this has two lines out of alignment with the rest of the contents. They have just one.

6. E. All the remaining symbols have contents of varying sizes, whereas this one has some that are the same.

7. A. It is the only one with the hair parted in the middle. Also, the others are pairs – B and D, C and E.

8. E. A and B, and C and D are pairs. B and D are A and C turned on their sides.

9. E. All the other symbols are left to right, mirror images.

10. D. The rest of the symbols are left to right, mirror images.

11. D. All the others follow the same, anti-clockwise ● ◊ ■ △ sequence.

12. E. The other symbols have identical contents:
    □□■, □▲, ◆

13. C. This symbol has two black squares to the left, instead of alternating with white ones as they do in the remaining symbols.

14. D. This symbol contains six sections; the other ones have four.

15. C. 'A' and 'E' are a pair. So too are 'B' and 'D'.

Continuing a Series of Symbols

1. D. The symbol is rotating clockwise. Keep turning this book around to check it!

2. D. The contents are rotating anti-clockwise. Watch the diamond moving backwards.

3. E. The ÷, −, ×, sequence suggests that − will follow the next ÷ ○●, ○● and ⤢, △, ⤢, △, and ●, ○, ●, ○ indicate that ○, ⤢ and ● will feature in the following symbol.

4. A. The alternate ⊕ (total), + (inside), ○ (outside) sequence of the first, third and fifth symbols indicates that the sequence of the second, fourth and sixth will be ⊟ (total), ⊖ (inside) and □ (outside).

5. B. The first and second symbols put together create the third. The fourth and fifth symbols appear to be going the other way, so you are looking for that missing bit!

6. E. The dots are moving back and forth; up and down.

7. E. The circle is swapping places with the other symbols, in a clockwise sequence.

8. D. The inner part of the symbol is moving clockwise, whilst the outside is revolving anti-clockwise.

9. B. The top inner symbol becomes the large outside one. The remaining inner symbols move up a position. The large outer symbol becomes the lowest inner one, and so on ...

10. C. The four squares to the left are rotating anti-clockwise. The two on the right remain static throughout.

11. E. The four outer symbols are turning in a clockwise direction. The one in the middle turns upside down and changes colour at successive moves.

12. B. The stripes are going backwards and forwards, up and down.

13. B. The symbols are moving clockwise, changing colour as they enter the top-right segment.

14. E. The symbol is rotating in a clockwise direction. Move the book around to confirm this!

15. D. The contents of the symbol are revolving clockwise, with the circle next to the arrow alternating its colour as it moves. Similarly, the arrows outside the symbol alternate positions at each turn.

3

Numerical
Ability Questions

Adding and Subtracting

1. 1005
2. 1335
3. 145
4. 278
5. 1045
6. 236
7. 161
8. 481
9. 755
10. 162
11. 4404
12. 34630
13. 3182
14. 63005
15. 2944
16. 26191
17. 4582
18. 46695
19. 2367
20. 89253
21. 886
22. 328
23. 273
24. 386
25. 367

26.	20
27.	188
28.	10
29.	163
30.	848
31.	1039
32.	112
33.	960
34.	95
35.	94
36.	245
37.	749
38.	575
39.	476
40.	113
41.	402
42.	238
43.	510
44.	184
45.	523
46.	142
47.	220
48.	351
49.	625
50.	215

Multiplying and Dividing

1. 5148
2. 78642
3. 267252
4. 3560
5. 0
6. 45221
7. 176562
8. 18942
9. 10659
10. 6100
11. 43
12. 77
13. 99
14. 68
15. 224
16. 82
17. 21
18. 82
19. 15
20. 7
21. 8
22. 34
23. 3310
24. 675
25. 81

26. 25
27. 60
28. 55
29. 304
30. ∞
31. 34
32. 147
33. 183
34. 88
35. 256
36. 7
37. 3
38. 140
39. 121
40. 72
41. 115
42. 111
43. 231
44. 448
45. 33
46. 361
47. 104
48. 121
49. 63
50. 141

Fractions and Percentages

1. 1
2. 10
3. 3
4. 5
5. 18
6. 6
7. 27
8. $\frac{11}{12}$
9. $1\frac{13}{20}$
10. $\frac{1}{10}$
11. $1\frac{5}{12}$
12. $3\frac{3}{5}$
13. $2\frac{2}{3}$
14. 6 $\times 13\frac{1}{2}$.
15. 48
16. 42
17. 3
18. 80
19. 60
20. 32
21. 15
22. 32
23. 1950
24. 72
25. 900

26. 140
27. 50
28. 30
29. 25
30. 77
31. 39
32. 240
33. 102
34. 72
35. 450
36. 360
37. 261
38. 210
39. 300
40. 1200
41. 900
42. 600
43. 450
44. 900
45. 30
46. 15
47. 50
48. 25
49. 40
50. 20

Continuing a Series of Numbers

1. 2 ($\div 4, \times 2, \div 4, \times 2, \div 4, \times 2$)
2. 26 ($- 3, + 6, - 3, + 6, - 3, + 6$)
3. 19 ($+ 2, + 1, + 2, + 1, + 2, + 1$)
4. 28 ($- 5, + 7, - 5, + 7, - 5, + 7$)
5. 148 ($+ 7, + 14, + 21, + 28, + 35, + 42$)
6. 9 ($+ 3, - 4, + 3, - 4, + 3, - 4$)
7. 9 ($+ 1, + 2, + 1, + 2, + 1, + 2$)
8. 16 ($- 0, + 2, - 0, + 2, - 0, + 2$)
9. 64 ($+ 3, + 6, + 9, + 12, + 15, + 18$)
10. 28 ($+ 2, + 3, + 4, + 5, + 6, + 7$)
11. 720 ($\times 1, \times 2, \times 3, \times 4, \times 5, \times 6$)
12. 3 ($\div 2, + 1, \div 2, + 1, \div 2, +1$)
13. 49 ($+ 3, + 5, + 7, + 9, + 11, + 13$)
14. 80 ($0 + 10 = 10, 10 + 10 = 20, 10 + 20 = 30$ etc.)
15. 248 ($\times 2 + 1, \times 5 + 2, \times 12 + 3$ etc.)
16. 29 ($+ 1, + 2, + 3, + 4, + 5, + 6$)
17. 2 ($- 1, \div 2, - 1, \div 2, - 1, \div 2$)
18. 30 ($+ 4, + 2, + 4, + 2, + 4, + 2$)
19. 8 ($\div 3, +5, \div 3, + 5, \div 3, + 5$)
20. 13 ($- 1, + 2, - 3, + 4, - 5, + 6$)
21. 55 ($+ 1, + 3, + 5, + 7, + 9, + 11$)
22. 45 ($- 3, \times 3, - 3, \times 3, - 3, \times 3$)
23. 18 ($- 3, + 6, - 3, + 6, - 3, + 6$)
24. 8 ($- 5, + 4, - 3, + 2, - 1, + 0$)
25. 27 ($\div 2, \times 3, \div 2, \times 3, \div 2, \times 3$)
26. 47 ($\times 2, + 1, \times 2, + 1, \times 2, + 1$)
27. 16 ($0 + 2 = 2, 2 + 2 = 4, 2 + 4 = 6$)
28. 184 ($\times 2 + 1, \times 2 + 2, \times 2 + 3$ etc.)
29. 39 ($3 + 3 = 6, 3 + 6 = 9, 6 + 9 = 15$ etc.)
30. 6562 ($\times 3 - 2, \times 3 - 2, \times 3 - 2$ etc.)

Numerical Awareness

1. 'Babytime'

1 'Sleepy Dreams' Cot	@	£149.95	£149.95	
2 'Teddies' Bumpers	@	£35.99	~~£70.98~~	£71.98
1 Cot Mattress	@	£45.00	£45.00	
1 Cot Pillow	@	£3.99	£3.99	
3 Stretch Sheets	@	£2.95	£8.85	
3 Pillow Cases	@	£1.99	£5.97	
2 Valances	@	£3.95	~~£7.99~~	£7.90
1 Teddy Bear	@	£12.99	£12.99	
		Total	~~£305.27~~	£306.63

2. 'Royal Oak'

2 Chilli Con Carne	@	£4.95	£9.90	
1 Lasagne	@	£4.50	£4.50	
2 Mixed Grills	@	£3.75	£7.50	
1 House Red	@	£6.95	£6.95	
1 House White	@	£6.95	~~£8.95~~	£6.95
3 Black Forest Gâteaus	@	£1.75	~~£4.25~~	£5.25
1 Apple Pie	@	£1.50	£1.50	
1 Chocolate Mousse	@	£1.99	£1.99	
3 Coffees	@	£0.70	~~£2.80~~	£2.10
2 Teas	@	£0.60	£1.20	
Subtotal			~~£47.58~~	£47.84
Service Charge	@	10%	~~£4.76~~	£4.78
		Total	~~£52.34~~	£52.62

3. 'Furniture World'

1 × 'Nathaniel' Dining Room Table	@	£339.95	£339.95	
2 × 'Nathaniel' Carver Chairs	@	£99.95	£199.90	
4 × 'Nathaniel' Dining Room Chairs	@	£79.99	~~£391.96~~	£319.96
1 × 'Gayfer' Wall Unit	@	£799.99	~~£799.95~~	£799.99
1 × 'Riseborough' CD Storage Unit	@	£46.25	£46.25	
1 × 'Diana' Recliner (Green)	@	£235.65	~~£265.65~~	£235.65
2 × Armchair Protectors	@	£3.99	£7.98	
1 × Footstool	@	£19.95	~~£19.99~~	£19.95
Subtotal			~~£2071.63~~	£1969.63
Discount @ 10%			~~£207.16~~	£196.96
Total			~~£1864.47~~	£1772.67

4. 'R & J Spares'

Quantity	Part Number	Unit Cost	Total	
2	AJX–3130	£2.99	£5.98	
3	AJX–3100	£3.95	~~£7.90~~	£11.85
2	AJX–3912	£4.90	£9.80	
3	BCM–4213	£2.95	£8.85	
1	BCM–4312	£3.99	£3.99	
5	NDR–2610	£2.95	£14.75	
2	NDR–2595	£2.99	£5.98	
3	AJX–3170	£4.99	~~£9.98~~	£14.97
3	AJX–3175	£4.95	~~£14.75~~	£14.85
2	AJX–3182	£4.95	~~£10.90~~	£9.90
Subtotal			~~£92.88~~	£102.92
Vat @ 17.5%			~~£16.25~~	£17.66
Total			~~£109.13~~	£120.58

5. 'Hollis Consultancy Services'

Date	Hours	Hourly Rate	Expenses	Total
15/4	4 (pm)	£24.95	–	£99.80
17/4	7 (am/pm)	£24.95	£15.00	£189.65
19/4	4 (am)	£24.95	–	£99.80
22/4	4 (pm)	£24.95	£12.95	£112.75
24/4	7 (am/pm)	£24.95	£15.00	£189.65
26/4	4 (am)	£24.95	–	£99.80
29/4	4 (pm)	£24.95	£12.95	£112.75
1/5	7 (am/pm)	£24.95	£15.00	£189.65
3/5	4 (pm)	£24.95	–	£99.80
Total				~~£1193.55~~ £1193.65

Numerical Estimation

1.

5 weeks	☐
6 weeks	⊟
7 weeks	⊟
8 weeks	☐
9 weeks	☐
10 weeks	☐

(2750 words per day $\times$ 4$\frac{1}{2}$ days per week = 12375 words)

(85,000-word book $\div$ 12375 words per week = 6.87 weeks)

2.

90 litres	☐
100 litres	☐
110 litres	⊟
120 litres	⊟
130 litres	☐
140 litres	☐

(221 + 108 + 323 + 77 + 103 + 189 = 1021 miles in total)

(1021 miles $\div$ 8.75 miles per litre = 116.69 litres)

3.

4 hours	☐
5 hours	☐
6 hours	⊟
7 hours	⊟
8 hours	☐
9 hours	☐

(33 essays × 12 minutes each = 396 minutes)
(396 minutes ÷ 60 minutes per hour = 6 hours, 36 minutes)

4.

£175	☐
£200	☐
£225	☐
£250	⊟
£275	⊟
£300	☐

(3 houses per hour × £2.50 each = £7.50 per hour)
(7.50 per hour × 7 hours each day = £52.50 per day)
(£52.50 per day × 5 days each week = £262.50 per week)

5.

5 weeks	☐
6 weeks	☐
7 weeks	⊟
8 weeks	⊟
9 weeks	☐
10 weeks	☐

(137 miles each day × 5 days per week = 685 miles each week)
(5000-mile service ÷ 685 miles per week = 7.3 weeks between services)

Numerical Checking

1.

Index	Sex	Age	Status	Index	Sex	Age	Status
00360	1	34	13/27	00360	1	34	13/27
00731	2	31	12/16	00731	2	31	12/16
00636	1	21	12/16	00366	1	21	12/16
01717	2	27	3/08	00717	2	26	3/08
00421	1	31	3/08	00421	1	31	3/08
00391	1	19	3/08	00391	1	19	13/08
10246	1	51	15/30	01246	1	41	15/30
00355	2	41	15/30	00335	2	51	15/30
00261	1	30	13/27	00261	1	30	15/30
01271	1	29	13/27	01271	1	29	13/27

2.

	Oct	Nov	Dec	Jan	Feb	Mar
Income	2000	2300	1700	2300	2000	1700
Expenditure	1800	1200	2000	1800	1200	2000
Balance	200	1100	–300	500	600	–300
Opening Bk. Bal.	500	700	1800	1500	2000	2800
Closing Bk. Bal.	700	1800	1700	2000	2800	2300

3.

a.	(3)6714	37610	32416
b.	46124	43123	47111
c.	41331	42164	49130
d.	37101	39121	34576
e.	33192	3921	39113
f.	42224	4136	43411
g.	51000	51603	58734
h.	43621	4326	44943
i.	33333	3173	34917
j.	26363	27319	24318
k.	33639	3391	38410
l.	44814	48418	44418

4.

	Apr	May	Jun	Jul	Aug	Sep
BAKER C.	37,132	39,246	30,003	31,626	39,414	42,413
MOFFAT P.	26,319	29,318	26,434	30,777	29,646	32,133
BENTINE M.	40,010	41,326	34,137	30,324	39,261	39,310
DALE J.	37,212	38,420	36,220	36,315	32,717	39,216
PERTWEE J.	50,200	38,701	43,230	44,455	45,424	38,321
CUSACK P.	24,190	24,004	26,270	29,321	31,331	28,711

5.

1.	27–1350	31–3160	31–3130	32–1360
2.	19–7217	14–7211	12–3015	19–4120
3.	18–7171	19–1171	13–1177	14–1177
4.	19–2641	23–9210	43–6121	22–6100
5.	31–3103	18–6141	21–9213	18–4341
6.	21–6666	71–9246	16–6666	11–2121
7.	27–9207	17–4222	33–4133	17–2882
8.	19–4164	13–7100	27–1200	19–1919
9.	18–8321	12–9210	41–9220	81–1818
10.	14–2381	13–1000	14–3369	77–7777

4
Spatial Ability
Answers

Fitting Shapes Together

1. B
2. C
3. A
4. C
5. A
6. A
7. D
8. A
9. B
10. E
11. C
12. D
13. D
14. A
15. B

Creating Solid Objects

1. D
2. A
3. C
4. D
5. C
6. B
7. D
8. C
9. A
10. A
11. A
12. D
13. A
14. C
15. A

Unfolding Solid Objects

1. A

2. B

3. B

4. D

5. C

6. D

7. B

8. A

9. B

10. A

11. A

12. C

13. C

14. A

15. A

Appendix 1: Useful Contacts

British Psychological Society, St Andrew's House, 48 Princess Road East, Leicester LE1 7DR – Tel: 01533 549568.

This is the leading body in the field of psychological testing, acting in both a regulatory and advisory manner. You should contact it for further guidance if you are to be successful at aptitude tests. Details of reputable test suppliers are available, on request.

Institute of Management, Management House, Cottingham Road, Corby, Northamptonshire NN17 1TT – Tel: 01536 204222.

An excellent source of information and advice on all key management issues, including selection testing. Its extensive reference library is particularly impressive, and is well worth accessing.

Institute of Personnel and Development, IPD House, Camp Road, Wimbledon, London SW19 4UX – Tel: 0181 946 9100.

The IPD is the UK's foremost organization in personnel management and related issues, such as recruitment and selection techniques. Do get in touch with it for more assistance on how to pass aptitude tests.

Mensa, Mensa House, St John's Square, Wolverhampton WV2 4IH – Tel: 01902 772771.

This society for highly intelligent people sets tests which are extremely similar to those you will be sitting during the selection process. It is worth applying for membership in order to be given the opportunity of a trial run on such comparable material. The society acts in an advisory and signposting capacity too.

NFER-Nelson, Darville House, 2 Oxford Road East, Windsor, Berkshire SL4 1DF – Tel: 01753 850333.

One of the UK's most renowned test suppliers – and well worth approaching for general guidance on this complex topic.

Appendix 2: Further Reading

Barrett, J. and Williams, G. *Test Your Own Aptitude*, Kogan Page Limited, 120 Pentonville Road, London N1 9JN Tel: 0171 278 0433. £6.99, paperback.

This interesting, self-help guide enables anyone seeking a job to check their personality and abilities and match their profile to a list of more than 400 careers to see which is most suited to them, and vice versa!

Bryon, Mike and Modha, Sanjay. *How to Pass Selection Tests*, Kogan Page Limited, 120 Pentonville Road, London N1 9JN Tel: 0171 278 0433. £6.99, paperback.

A clear and informative guide to different types of selection test, and how to tackle them successfully. The book contains useful examples and illustrative material.

Bryon, Mike and Modha, Sanjay. *How to Pass Technical Selection Tests*, Kogan Page Limited, 120 Pentonville Road, London N1 9JN Tel: 0171 278 0433. £6.99, paperback.

Aimed at people seeking employment in a technical field, this book covers the most likely selection tests to be faced by them during their search. It is supported by practice material.

Modha, Sanjay. *How to Pass Computer Selection Tests*, Kogan Page Limited, 120 Pentonville Road, London N1 9JN Tel: 0171 278 0433. £7.99, paperback.

Written for people seeking work in the computing field, this book takes a broad look at a wide range of selection tests, and incorporates a mass of practice material.

Toplis, John, Dulewicz, Vic and Fletcher, Clive. *Psychological Testing: A Manager's Guide*, Institute of Personnel and Development, IPD House, Camp Road, Wimbledon, London SW19 4UX Tel: 0181 9469100. £11.95, paperback.

A practical and comprehensive guide to selecting pyschological tests for use in recruitment and staff appraisal. It can be helpful to see testing from the opposite viewpoint before tests are tackled.

Also available from Thorsons:
How to Win at Aptitude Tests Paul Pelshenke

How to Win at Aptitude Tests

Volume II